THE YEAR Y WERE BOR

1940

A fascinating book about the year 1940 with information on History of Britain, Events of the year USA, Adverts of 1940, Cost of living, Births, Sporting events, Book publications, Movies, Music, World events and People in power.

INDEX

HISTORY OF AMERICA IN 1940

In the summer of 1940 Adolf Hitler could have won the Second World War. He came close to that. Had he won, we would be living in a world so different as to be hardly imaginable. So let us contemplate that dangerous summer. It was then that the shape of the world in which we now live began to take form.

There was a curious, abstract quality to the Second World War when it started. On the first day of September in 1939, Hitler's armies invaded Poland. In 1914 the Germans had gone to war not knowing what the British would do. In 1939 the British had given Poland a guarantee to deter Hitler, to make it clear that a German attack on Poland would mean a British (and a French) declaration of war against Germany. Until the last minute Hitler hoped that the British did not mean what they said. In a way he was right. The British and the French governments kept their word and declared war nearly three days after the German armies had driven into Poland. Yet the British and French armies did virtually nothing.

Before long the phrase "Phony War," invented by American journalists, came into the language. Poland was overrun: but in this war, it really was All Quiet on the Western Front. The French and the British troops spent the freezing winter that followed standing still, the French occasionally peering across the wooded German frontier from the concrete casemates of the Maginot Line. If not a phony war, it was a reluctant one.

There was a curious, abstract quality in the mood of the American people too. When the First World War broke out in Europe, not one in ten thousand Americans thought that their country would ever become involved in it. In 1914 the American people and their President, Woodrow Wilson, took a naive kind of pride in their neutrality.

When, on September 3, 1939, Franklin Roosevelt addressed the American people, he said the United States would stay neutral: but Roosevelt then added that he could not "ask that every American remain neutral in thought as well." Most Americans were not. They abhorred Hitler, yet they had no desire to commit themselves on the side of Britain or France or Poland. They followed the conflict on their radios: it was exciting to hear the voices of famous correspondents crackling through the transatlantic ether from the blacked-out capitals of a Europe at war. Many Americans uneasily felt—felt, rather than said—that sooner or later their country would become involved in the war. They did not look forward to it.

Besides, the Phony War got curiouser and curiouser. It had started between Germany and Poland and Britain and France; but three months later the only fighting that was going on occurred in the snowy forests of Finland, a winter war between Finland and Russia. American sympathies for Finland arose. The British government noticed this. It was toying with the idea of coming to the aid of Finland, for many reasons, including the purpose of impressing American opinion. But the winter war came to an end. Churchill now wished to open a far-flung front against Germany, in Norway. Hitler forestalled him. On a freezing, raw morning in early April, his troops invaded Denmark and Norway. They conquered Denmark in a few hours and Norway in a few weeks.

Hitler's triumph in Norway—which he conquered nearly undisturbed by the British navy and largely unvexed by the hapless Allied troops put ashore and then withdrawn again—had an unexpected effect. The great portly figure of his nemesis had arisen—an old-fashioned figure of a man, whose very appearance rose like a spectral monument out of the historical mist. As a member of the Chamberlain government, Winston Churchill had been responsible for much of the Norwegian fiasco. Yet the representatives of the British people had had enough of Chamberlain's reluctant warfare. They helped Winston Churchill into the saddle of the prime minister ship—by coincidence, on the very day when the German onslaught in Western Europe had begun.

It was the first of several great coincidences that summer: the kind of coincidences that people weaned on scientific logic dislike and others, with a touch of poetry in their souls, love. Or as the great Portuguese proverb says: God writes straight with crooked lines. But, as often happens in this world, we see the meaning only in retrospect. At the time, there was no guarantee that Churchill would last. He could have disappeared after a few weeks: a brave, old-fashioned orator, overtaken by the surging tide of the twentieth century, swept under by the wave of the future. When his horse is shot out under him, the best rider must fall.

On the tenth of May, at dawn—it was a radiant, beautiful morning, cloudless across Europe from the Irish Sea to the Baltic—Hitler flung his armies forward. They were the winged carriers of an astonishing drama. Holland fell in five days; Belgium in eighteen. Two days after the German drive had begun, the French front was broken. Another eight days, and the Germans reached the Channel. Calais and Boulogne fell. Dunkirk held for just ten days. Most of the British Expeditionary Force barely escaped; all their equipment was lost. Five weeks from the day they had started westward, German regiments were marching down the Champs Elysées. Three more days, and a new French government asked for surrender.

Here was a drama of forty days unequaled in the history of war for centuries, even by the brilliant victories of Napoleon. Hitler himself had a hand in designing that most astonishing of successful campaigns. He also had a hand in designing an armistice that the French would be inclined to accept.

He hoped that the United States would stay out of the war. His propaganda minister Joseph Goebbels ordered the toning down of anti-American items in the German press and radio. When the German army marched into an empty Paris, its commanders made a courtesy call on the American ambassador, who, alone among the envoys of the Great Powers, chose to stay in the capital instead of following the torn French government during its sorry flight to the south. The Hotel Grillon, headquarters of the German military command, was across the street from the American Embassy. The German general in charge received the American military and naval attachés at ten in the morning. He offered them glasses of what he described as "the very best brandy in the Grillon." His staff approached the American ambassador with calculated and self-conscious courtesies, to which William C. Bullitt responded with all the tact and reserve of a great envoy of classical stamp. Two months later Bullitt was back from France in his native city of Philadelphia, where, in front of Independence Hall, he made a stirring speech, calling the American people to rally to the British side against Hitler. His speech did not have much of a popular echo.

Hitler hoped that the British would think twice before going on with the war. Their chances, he said, were hopeless; and he repeated that he had no quarrel with the existence of the British Empire. He hoped that the British would make some kind of peace with him.

They didn't. Their savior Churchill had arisen; and behind Churchill—slowly, cautiously, but deliberately—rose the massive shadow of Franklin Roosevelt. In the summer of 1940—still a year and a half before Pearl Harbor and his declaration of war against the United States—Hitler already knew that his principal enemy was Roosevelt, whom he came to hate with a fury even greater than his hatred for Churchill (and, of course, for Stalin, whom he admired in many ways till the end).

Roosevelt and Churchill knew each other. More than that, they had, for some time, put their hopes in each other. For some time Franklin Roosevelt—secretly, privately, through some of his envoys, personal friends whom he trusted—had encouraged those men in London and Paris who were convinced that Hitler had to be fought. Foremost among these was Winston Churchill. In turn, Churchill knew what Roosevelt thought of Hitler; and he knew that what Britain needed was the support of the giant United States. The two men had begun to correspond, in secret. On the day German armor appeared on the cliffs across from Dover, an American citizen, an employee of the American Embassy in London, was arrested by detectives of Scotland Yard.

During that beautiful and deadly early summer of 1940, Franklin Roosevelt, too, had to contend with a difficult problem. This was the divided mind of the American people. We have heard much lately—because of nostalgic inclinations due to the trauma of a divided nation during the Vietnam War—about the Second World War having been a Good War, when this giant nation was united in purpose and in concept. Even after Pearl Harbor this was not exactly true. During the summer of 1940 it was not true at all. There was a small minority of Americans that was convinced the United States should abet and aid the nations warring against Hitler at almost any price. There was another, larger, minority of isolationists that wanted the United States to keep out of this war, at all costs. And there was a large and inchoate majority that did not like Hitler and that was contemptuous of the Japanese, but their minds were divided: yes, the United States should oppose the enemies of democracy; no, the democracy of the United States should not engage in a foreign war. There were people who understood that these sentiments were contradictory. Others did not. Yet other Americans began to change their minds—slowly, gradually, at times imperceptibly. But not until after the dangerous summer of 1940.

There was a strange unreality in the American scene during the early summer. The few people from Europe and Britain who landed in New York during those dazzling May and June days found themselves in quite another world—in the gleaming lobbies of the great New York hotels, among the glistening stream of automobiles and taxis, before the glowing glass windows of the incredibly rich department stores, around which flowed the masses of a confident, prosperous, largely undisturbed American people. It was as if the astonishing speed of the devolving events in Western Europe was too fast to grasp. It was not until the fall of France that the startling new specter of a German Europe cohered.

Even after the fall of France, he believed, and said, that "naval power was the key to history," that Hitler, because of his naval inferiority, was bound to lose this war. For the European theater, this was wrong in the long run. The internal-combustion engine had changed the nature of warfare; for the first time in five hundred years, armies could move faster on land than on the seas. Eventually Hitler's armies had to be destroyed on land, and mostly by the Russians. Had the German armies not been chewed up by the Russians, the Western allies, with all of their sea and air superiority, could not have invaded France in 1944.

What is more important, Roosevelt was wrong in the short run too. If worst came to worst, he thought, and told Churchill, the British navy could come across the Atlantic to fight on. But Churchill could not guarantee that. As early as May 15 he wrote Roosevelt that if American help came too late, "the weight may be more than we can bear." Five days later, when the Germans had reached the Channel, he repeated this: "If members of this administration were finished and others came in to parley amid the ruins, you must not be blind to the fact that the sole remaining bargaining counter with Germany would be the fleet, and if this country was left by the United States to its fate no one would have the right to blame those then responsible if they made the best terms they could for the surviving inhabitants." The day after Paris fell, Churchill let Roosevelt know that "a point may be reached in the struggle where the present ministers no longer have control of affairs and when very easy terms could be obtained for the British Islands by their becoming a vassal state of the Hitler empire." This was exactly what Hitler had in mind. As in the case of France, his plan called for a partial occupation of the British island, with the fleet in British ports but demobilized, and with a Germanophile British government somewhere within the reach of the German occupation forces.

He had to prepare himself for an unprecedented nomination for an unprecedented third-term election as President. And against him a new American coalition had begun to gather: it came to be called America First, composed by all kinds of men and women who thought, and said, that American support to Britain was illegal, futile, and wrong. A leader of this movement was Charles A. Lindbergh, a great American hero. Its actual members were recognizable, while its potential popularity was not measurable. It is wrong to consider America First as if it had been a fluke, a conventicle of reactionaries and extremists. There were all kinds of respectable Americans who opposed Roosevelt and who were loath to engage themselves on the British side. They included not only Herbert Hoover but John Foster Dulles, with whom the Lindbergh's were dining on the evening the French asked for an armistice—in other words, surrender.

Then came the second great coincidence. On the twenty-second of June the French delegates signed their capitulation to Hitler. It was his greatest triumph—and the lowest point in Britain's fortunes in a thousand years. Yet, that very week, the British cause was lifted by an unexpected stroke of fortune, in Philadelphia of all places. There the Republican party had met in convention and nominated Wendell Willkie for their presidential candidate: and Willkie was not an isolationist. There had been many reasons to believe that the Republicans would nominate an isolationist: perhaps Robert A. Taft from Ohio or Arthur H. Vandenberg from Michigan. The Midwest, with its large German-American and Scandinavian-American populations, mostly Republicans, was strongly isolationist. Willkie came from Indiana; and after Hitler's invasion of Scandinavia, some of that Scandinavian-American Anglophobe isolationism began to melt away. Yet the isolationist conviction was still a strong, channeled current among the milling Republican delegates on the floor, in that boiling arena of Philadelphia's Convention Hall. But a carefully orchestrated and arranged effort, with the galleries chanting, "We want Willkie," carried the day.

Hitler now dawdled—for one of the very few times during the war. Europe lay at his feet. He went off on a vacation, touring places in northern France where he had soldiered during the First World War. He made a short, furtive visit to an empty Paris at dawn. He suggested a European version of the Monroe Doctrine: Europe for the "Europeans," America for the Americans. He did not draft the directive for the invasion of Britain until the middle of July—and even then with some reluctance. On July 19 he made a long and crude speech, offering a last chance of peace to Britain. In London the German "peace offer" was let drop with an icy silence, somewhat like a blackmailing note left at the door of a proud old mansion.

Six weeks had now passed since France had fallen; and Britain still stood, inviolate, increasingly aglow with the spirit breathed by Churchill's words. Franklin Roosevelt made up his mind. He took an important step. He brought in a few confidants who assured him that he, in his constitutional capacity as Commander-in-Chief, could go ahead. This was at the very end of July. Two days later Roosevelt announced to his cabinet that the United States would "sell directly or indirectly fifty or sixty old World War destroyers to Great Britain." Churchill had asked for such a deal in May. The destroyers were not, in themselves, as important as the gesture, the meaning of the act itself for the world. It meant the decisive departure from American neutrality. What Roosevelt did not know, and what Churchill did not know, was that, at the same moment, Hitler had taken his first decisive move in ordering the German army staff to plan for an invasion of Russia.

There was method in Hitler's madness. What did he say to the close circle of his commanders on that day? "England's hope is Russia and America." Against America he could do nothing. But "if hope in Russia is eliminated, America is also eliminated," he said. He was not altogether wrong. Eliminating Russia would destroy British hopes for an eventual conquest of Germany in Europe, and it would strengthen Japan's position in the Far East. In the United States it would also strengthen popular opposition to Roosevelt. There were many Americans who hated and feared communism: the elimination of communist Russia would make Roosevelt's continued intervention on the side of Britain increasingly futile and unpopular.

Air warfare against England was about to begin; but "if results of the air war are not satisfactory, [invasion] preparations will be halted." So at the end of July 1940, Hitler, after some hesitation, began to consider invading Russia at the very moment when Roosevelt, after some hesitation, made his decision to commit the United States on the British side.

This last day of July in 1940 was not merely an important milestone. It was the turning point of the Second World War. There followed the climax of the Battle of Britain in the air, which, for Hitler, was indecisive. So far as the American people went, the bombing of Britain solidified their gradually crystallizing inclination to stand by the British. Britain held out; and in November 1940 Roosevelt easily won the majority of his people for a third term

What followed—Lend-Lease, the Selective Service Bill, the Marines sent to Greenland and Iceland, Roosevelt's order to the Navy to shoot at any appearance of Axis naval craft—was a foregone conclusion. Hitler was shrewd enough to order German commanders to avoid incidents with the United States at all costs. He did not want to furnish Roosevelt with the pretext of a serious naval incident. Eventually his Japanese allies were to accomplish what he was reluctant to do. Five hundred days after that thirty-first of July came another great coincidence. In the snow-covered wasteland before Moscow, the Russians halted the German army just when, in the sunny wastes of the Pacific, the Japanese attack on Pearl Harbor propelled the United States into the war. The Germans and the Japanese would achieve astounding victories even after that: but the war they could not win.

One year before Pearl Harbor, Roosevelt had announced that the United States would be the "arsenal of democracy." Churchill had told the American people: "Give us the tools, and we will finish the job." Did he mean this? We cannot tell. It was far from certain that Hitler could be defeated by the supply of American armaments alone. What was needed was the employment of immense American armies and navies in the field. And even that would not be enough. Hitler's defeat could not be accomplished without the armed might of Russia, whereby victory in Europe had to be shared with Russia.

Forty-six years later we have a government that neither remembers nor understands this. Churchill understood the alternative: either all of Europe ruled by Germany, or the eastern portion of it controlled by Russia. It was not a pleasant alternative. In world politics few alternatives are altogether pleasant. Yet half of Europe was better than none. Had it not been for Franklin Roosevelt during that dangerous summer of 1940, even this alternative would have been moot. Had the United States been led by an isolationist president in 1940, Hitler would have won the war.

U.S. EVENTS OF 1940

February

7th Pinocchio was released in 1940. It was an American animated musical fantasy film produced by Walt Disney Productions, distributed by RKO Radio Pictures and was based on the Italian children's novel The Adventures of Pinocchio by Carlo Collodi. It was the second animated feature film produced by Disney, made after the first animated success of Snow White and the Seven Dwarfs (1937).

10th Puss Gets the Boot is an American one-reel animated cartoon and is the first short in what would become the Tom and Jerry cartoon series. It was directed by William Hanna, Joseph Barbera and Rudolf Ising, and produced by Rudolf Ising and Fred Quimby. As was the practice of MGM shorts at the time, only Rudolf Ising is credited. It was released to theaters on February 10, 1940 by Metro-Goldwyn-Mayer.

27th Carbon-14 (14C), or radiocarbon, is a radioactive isotope of carbon with an atomic nucleus containing 6 protons and 8 neutrons. Its presence in organic materials is the basis of the radiocarbon dating method pioneered by Willard Libby and colleagues (1949) to date archaeological, geological and hydrogeological samples. Carbon-14 was discovered on February 27, 1940, by Martin Kamen and Sam Ruben at the University of California Radiation Laboratory in Berkeley, California.

March

2nd Elmer's Candid Camera was a Merrie Melodies cartoon short directed by Chuck Jones, and first released on March 2, 1940, by Warner Bros. It marks the first appearance of a redesigned Elmer Fudd (voiced by Arthur Q. Bryan), and the fourth appearance of the prototype rabbit that would later evolve into Bugs Bunny (voiced by Mel Blanc).

23rd Truth or Consequences debuts on NBC Radio. Ralph Edwards stated he got the idea for a new radio program from a favorite childhood parlor game, "Forfeits". The show premiered on NBC Radio in March 23, 1940, and was an instant hit with listeners.

Truth or Consequences was the first game show to air on broadcast television, airing as a one-time experiment on the first day of New York station WNBT's commercial program schedule on July 1, 1941. However, the series did not appear on TV again until 1950, when the medium had caught on commercially

April

1st April Fools' Day is also the census date for the 16th U.S. Census.

4th Dick Grayson (AKA as Robin, the Boy Wonder) first appears with Batman.

7th Booker T. Washington becomes the first African American to be depicted on a United States postage stamp

12th Opening day at Jamaica Racetrack features the use of pari-mutuel betting equipment, a departure from bookmaking heretofore used exclusively throughout New York state. Other NY tracks follow suit later in 1940.

April

21st The $64,000 Question had its roots in the CBS radio quiz show, Take It or Leave It, which followed in the wake of the pioneering Professor Quiz (radio's first quiz program) and Uncle Jim's Question Bee (the second radio quiz show). Take It or Leave It ran from April 21, 1940 to July 27, 1947. It was first hosted by Bob Hawk (1940–41), followed by Phil Baker (1941–47).

23rd The Rhythm Club fire (or The Natchez Dance Hall Holocaust) was a fire in a dance hall in Natchez, Mississippi, on the night of April 23, 1940, which killed 209 people and severely injured many others. Hundreds of people were trapped inside the building. At the time, it was the second deadliest building fire in the history of the nation. It is now ranked as the fourth deadliest assembly and club fire in U.S. history. The dance hall, a converted blacksmith shop once used as a church, was located in a one-story steel-clad wood-frame building at 1 St. Catherine Street, blocks from the city's business district.

It was a single-story, wood building with corrugated steel siding that was 120 ft (36.6m) x 38 ft (11.6 m) with 24 windows that were mostly shuttered or nailed shut at the time of the fire. There was only one exit, with an inward opening door, that opened into a main entrance foyer that had another set of doors that also opened inward.

May

15th The very first McDonald's restaurant opens in San Bernardino, California. Founded in May 15, 1940 as a restaurant operated by Richard and Maurice McDonald, in San Bernardino, California, United States. They rechristened their business as a hamburger stand, and later turned the company into a franchise, with the Golden Arches logo being introduced in 1953 at a location in Phoenix, Arizona. In 1955, Ray Kroc, a businessman, joined the company as a franchise agent and proceeded to purchase the chain from the McDonald brothers. McDonald's is the world's largest restaurant chain by revenue, serving over 69 million customers daily in over 100 countries across 37,855 outlets as of 2018.

Women's stockings made of nylon are first placed on sale across the U.S. Almost five million pairs are bought on this day.

16th U.S. President Franklin D. Roosevelt, addressing a joint session of Congress, asks for an extraordinary credit of approximately $900 million to finance construction of at least 50,000 airplanes per year.

18th The 6.9 Mw El Centro earthquake affects California's Imperial Valley with a maximum Mercalli intensity of X (Extreme), causing nine deaths and twenty injuries. Financial losses are around $6 million. Significant damage also occurs in Mexicali, Mexico.

25th The Crypt of Civilization at Oglethorpe University is sealed. The Crypt of Civilization is a sealed airtight chamber built between 1937 and 1940 at Oglethorpe University in Brookhaven, Georgia, in Metro Atlanta. The 2,000-cubic-foot (57 m3) room contains numerous artifacts and documents, and is designed for opening in the year 8113 AD. During the 50th anniversary year of its sealing, the Guinness Book of World Records cited the crypt as the "first successful attempt to bury a record of this culture for any future inhabitants or visitors to the planet Earth.

29th The Vought XF4U-1, prototype of the F4U Corsair U.S. fighter later used in WWII, makes its first flight.

June

10th | U.S. President Franklin D. Roosevelt denounces Italy's actions with his "Stab in the Back" speech during the graduation ceremonies of the University of Virginia.

14th | U.S. President Franklin D. Roosevelt signs the Naval Expansion Act into law, which aims to increase the United States Navy's tonnage by 11%.

24th | U.S. politics: The Republican Party begins its national convention in Philadelphia and nominates Wendell Willkie as its candidate for president.

July

1st | The 1940 Tacoma Narrows Bridge, the first Tacoma Narrows Bridge, was a suspension bridge in the U.S. state of Washington that spanned the Tacoma Narrows strait of Puget Sound between Tacoma and the Kitsap Peninsula. It opened to traffic on July 1, 1940, and dramatically collapsed into Puget Sound on November 7 the same year. This is probably the biggest and most famous non-fatal engineering disaster in U.S. history. Throughout its short existence, it was the world's third-longest suspension bridge by main span, behind the Golden Gate Bridge and the George Washington Bridge.

July

15th | U.S. politics: The Democratic Party begins its national convention in Chicago and nominates Franklin D. Roosevelt for an unprecedented third term as president.

20th | The Arroyo Seco Parkway, one of the first freeways built in the U.S., opens to traffic, connecting downtown Los Angeles with Pasadena, California.

27th | Bugs Bunny makes his debut in the Oscar-nominated cartoon short, A Wild Hare.

August

4th | Gen. John J. Pershing, in a nationwide radio broadcast, urges all-out aid to Britain in order to defend the Americas, while Charles Lindbergh speaks to an isolationist rally at Soldier Field in Chicago.

September

1st The U.S. Army 45th Infantry Division (previously a National Guard Division in Arizona, Colorado, New Mexico and Oklahoma), is activated and ordered into federal service for 1 year, to engage in a training program in Ft. Sill and Louisiana, prior to serving in World War II.

2nd WWII: An agreement between America and Great Britain is announced to the effect that 50 U.S. destroyers needed for escort work will be transferred to Great Britain. In return, America gains 99-year leases on British bases in the North Atlantic, West Indies and Bermuda.

12th The Hercules Munitions Plant in Succasunna-Kenvil, New Jersey explodes, killing 55 people.

16th WWII: The Selective Training and Service Act of 1940 are signed into law by Franklin D. Roosevelt, creating the first peacetime draft in U.S. history.

26th WWII: The United States imposes a total embargo on all scrap metal shipments to Japan.

October

1st The first section of the Pennsylvania Turnpike, the country's first long-distance controlled-access highway, is opened between Irwin and Carlisle.

16th The draft registration of approximately 16 million men begins in the United States.

29th The Selective Service System lottery is held in Washington, D.C.

November

5th U.S. presidential election, 1940: Democrat incumbent Franklin D. Roosevelt defeats Republican challenger Wendell Willkie and becomes the nation's first and only third-term president.

7th In Tacoma, Washington, the Tacoma Narrows Bridge (nicknamed the "Galloping Gertie") collapses in a 42-mile-per-hour (68 km/h) wind storm, causing the center span of the bridge to sway. When it collapses, a 600-foot-long (180 m) design of the center span falls 190 feet above the water, killing Tubby, a black male cocker spaniel dog.

11th The Armistice Day Blizzard (or the Armistice Day Storm) took place in the Midwest region of the United States on November 11 (Armistice Day) and November 12, 1940. The intense early-season "panhandle hook" winter storm cut a 1,000-mile-wide (1600 km) swath through the middle of the country from Kansas to Michigan.

13th Walt Disney's Fantasia is released. It is the first box office failure for Disney, though it recoups its cost years later and becomes one of the most highly regarded of Disney's films.

16th An unexploded pipe bomb is found in the Consolidated Edison office building (only years later is the culprit, George Metesky, apprehended).

December

8th The Chicago Bears, in what will become the most one-sided victory in National Football League history, defeat the Washington Redskins 73–0 in the 1940 NFL Championship Game.

17th President Franklin D. Roosevelt, at his regular press conference, first sets forth the outline of his plan to send aid to Great Britain that will become known as Lend-Lease. The Lend-Lease policy was a program under which the United States supplied the United Kingdom (and British Commonwealth); Free France, the Republic of China, and later the Soviet Union and other Allied nations with food, oil, and materiel between 1941 and August 1945. This included warships and warplanes, along with other weaponry. It was signed into law on March 11, 1941, and ended in September 1945. In general the aid was free, although some hardware (such as ships) were returned after the war. In return, the U.S. was given leases on army and naval bases in Allied territory during the war. Canada operated a similar smaller program called Mutual Aid.

20th The 5.3 Mw New Hampshire earthquake shakes New England with a maximum Mercalli intensity of VII (Very strong). This first event in a doublet earthquake is followed four days later by a 5.6 Mw shock. Total damage from the events is light.

29th Franklin D. Roosevelt, in a fireside chat to the nation, declares that the United States must become "the great arsenal of democracy."

30th California's first modern freeway, the future State Route 110, opens to traffic in Pasadena, California, as the Arroyo Seco Parkway (now the Pasadena Freeway).

You don't have to be told

It's the yarn you can tell on any beach —as far as you can see it. Nothing else could perform this small miracle of fit with freedom, of control with comfort. This suave technique has made the American bathing beauty the envy of the world. When choosing a suit remember that the stretch of "Lastex" yarn is applied with equal facility to any sort of woven or knitted fabric, silk or cotton, wool or rayon. That in many and various applications it glorifies every type of suit, maillot, skirted or dressmaker. There is a swimsuit made with this priceless ingredient to fit every kind of figure, and at a price to fit every kind of purse. So the rest is up to you. Just ask for a suit made with "Lastex" yarn at the stores you usually patronize, under the name of a favorite maker, if you like. But be sure *your* suit is made with benefit of fashion's fourth dimension.

Lastex
REG. U. S. PAT. OFF.

THE MIRACLE YARN THAT MAKES THINGS FIT

An elastic yarn manufactured exclusively by United States Rubber Company, Rockefeller Center, New York City

"LAUGH, Miss LOY!"

Even after "turning on a laugh" 100 times a day, Myrna Loy*—MGM star—finds Luckies easy on her throat..

A word about your throat— "Laughing before the sound camera is hard on the throat," says Myrna Loy. "After scenes of this sort, it's clear that Luckies are *the* cigarette for anyone who wants a light smoke that's easy on the throat!" Here's the reason in a nut-shell: the process "It's Toasted" takes out certain irritants that are found in *all* tobacco!

A word about tobacco—Aren't men who spend their lives buying and selling tobacco the best judges of tobacco quality? Then remember ...sworn records reveal that among independent tobacco experts Lucky Strike has *twice* as many exclusive smokers as all other brands combined. With men who know tobacco best—it's Luckies—2 to 1.

*STAR OF MGM PICTURE "MAN-PROOF"

Luckies—A Light Smoke

Easy on your throat—"It's Toasted"

WITH MEN WHO KNOW TOBACCO BEST
It's Luckies 2 to 1

Copyright 1937, The American Tobacco Company

17

"WHAT ARE THE WILD WAVES SAYING?"
TRY BEECHAM'S PILLS.

THE WORLD'S MEDICINE.

From the earliest days of medicinal science no antidote has achieved such a reputation as
BEECHAM'S PILLS.

Their fame has reached the uttermost parts of the earth; their curative power is universally acknowledged to a degree unprecedented in the annals of physical research; and it is echoed from shore to shore that for Bilious and Nervous Disorders, Indigestion with its dreaded allies, and for assisting Nature in her wondrous functions, they are

WORTH A GUINEA A BOX.

Gibson

Electric Spanish Guitars
← ES-250 Model

● IN THE ES-250 MODEL, Gibson has created the best electric Spanish guitar possible to make. The lightest touch on its strings can be amplified to any volume you desire. A touch on the tone control and you change the tonal color from a rich bass to a brilliant treble. A really great guitar.

Body size 17" wide and 21" long—Advanced size like the L-7 and L-5—curly maple back and rim—maple neck—spruce top—rosewood fingerboard—chocolate brown finish with golden sunburst shading on top and back—fingerboard and peghead inlaid with attractive pearl designs—white, black and white ivoroid binding on top of body and fingerrest—white ivoroid binding on bottom of body and fingerboard—elevated brown celluloid fingerrest—side position marks—rosewood adjustable bridge—new Kluson "Seal-Fast" nickel individual machine heads—modern nickel extension tailpiece—19 frets—Exclusive Gibson Adjustable Truss Rod neck construction.

This instrument has built-in individually balanced tone generator unit bound with white, black and white celluloid. It has separate chrome plated pole pieces for each string, giving maximum in tonal reproduction. Tone and volume controls are on one side. The extra strong shielded cord is 15 feet. Plugs and spring protectors are shielded nickel.

PRICE (instrument and cord) $150.00

CASE: No. 600—Heavy faultless construction, covered with brown waterproof aeroplane cloth to match amplifier—sturdy luggage catches—American Beauty silk plush lining. Price: $28.00.

ZIPPER CASE COVER: Tan waterproof zipper cover with leather bindings and metal bumpers. $15.00.

AMPLIFIERS
The ES-250 and ES-150 instruments are to be used with EH-185 or EH-150 Amplifiers.

Electric Tenor Guitar

Style EST-150. Same as ES-150 but with Four String Tenor Neck and Fingerboard. 15 foot cord. $77.50.
CASE: No. 534—$16.50.

ES-150 CASE: No. 534 — Aeroplane Cloth covering — heavy Faultless construction — purple flannel lining. $16.50. ZIPPER CASE COVER: Tan zipper waterproof cover — leather bindings—metal bumpers. $15.00.

ES-150 illustrated with EH-185 Amplifier

ES-150 MODEL →

Grand auditorium body—carved spruce top—northern maple back and rim—mahogany neck and rosewood fingerboard—chocolate brown finish with golden sunburst—white ivoroid binding on top and bottom of body and fingerboard—ebony adjustable bridge—brown celluloid fingerrest bound with white ivoroid—individual nickel machine heads—nickel plated extension tailpiece—pearl inlays in fingerboard and peghead—side position dots—exclusive Gibson adjustable Truss Rod neck construction, and 19 frets. Entire tone generator unit built inside guitar body. Tone and volume controls conveniently placed for instant regulation.

Price (instrument and 15-foot cord) $77.50

THE GREATEST ENGINE IN THE LOW-PRICE FIELD!

8 cylinders . . . 85 horsepower . . .
built with such amazing accuracy it needs no "breaking-in"

GREATEST because it has *eight* cylinders. America's finest, highest priced cars *all* have at least eight cylinders!

GREATEST because of its efficient V-type design. V-type engines hold world's records on land, sea, and in the air!

GREATEST because of the economy it delivers. In the 1940 Gilmore-Yosemite Economy Run, the Ford V-8 topped all standard-drive cars in its class with an average of 24.92 miles on each gallon of gas!

GREATEST because of the accuracy with which it's built. Other engines have to be "babied" along for 500 or 1000 miles. But you can drive your Ford V-8 sixty miles an hour the day it's delivered!

ONLY an eight-cylinder engine can give you smooth eight-cylinder performance! And only the big, roomy Ford V-8 gives you such performance at a low price! *Once you've felt the eight Ford cylinders flashing underfoot, you'll never be satisfied with anything less!*

FORD V·8

COST OF LIVING 1940

Wages	$1,725.00
House price	$3,920.00
House rental	$30.00 per month
New Car	$850.00
Gallon of gas	11 cents
Battery for torch	10 cents
Loaf of bread	10 cents
Campbell's tomato soup	25 cents for 3 cans
Chewing Gum	12 cents for 3
Flour	25 cents for 5 pound bag
Fresh Chicken	55 cents a pound
Radio	$16.95
Hoover	$52.50
Automatic washing machine	$249.99
Frigidaire Electric Cooker range	$179.95
Hearing Aid	$59.99

Toys

Vintage 1940s 98 Cents Toys
Price: 98 cents
Description: A selection costing 98 cents including Anti-Aircraft Gun on back of Army Truck, Tractor and Trailer, Dump Truck and Car Transporter Wagon, they are all between 12 and 18 inches long and made of steel.

1940s Blackbird Crystal Set
Price: $2.98
Description: Blackbird Crystal Set, picks up stations up to 75 miles away, use an earphone to listen to, comes with a 75ft aerial and 25ft ground wire.

Magnavox Modular Television Receiver correlated with Magnavox Cosmopolitan Radio-Phono

NOW! Magnavox big-picture television for only $279⁵⁰

America's greatest value! Finest at any price—with all the great innovations of MAGNASCOPE Television System • CLEAREST PICTURES—*sharpest contrast* • NO EYESTRAIN—*built-in filter eliminates glare and flicker* • EASIEST PROGRAM SELECTION—*switch to programs you want instead of tuning for them* • AUTOMATIC PICTURE STABILIZER *holds picture steady* • EXTRA POWER—*"reaches" for distance* • HIGHEST-FIDELITY SOUND—*world-famous Magnavox speakers* • FINEST FURNITURE.

DON'T deprive your family of the entertainment television offers. Since Magnavox brings you the finest for so little money, don't be satisfied with anything less.

See your Magnavox dealer and make your selection now. His name is in the classified telephone directory. The Magnavox Co., Fort Wayne 4, Ind.

Television Facts And Fun

Let author-playwright George B. Anderson tell you about television and what it did for his family. Liberally illustrated new book, "More Fun For Your Money With Magnavox Television" free on request. Mail coupon today!

the magnificent
Magnavox
television - radio - phonograph

Prices subject to change without notice

THE MAGNAVOX COMPANY
2133 Buster Road
Fort Wayne 4, Indiana

Without obligation please send me George B. Anderson's new book on television.

Name_____

Address_____

City_____ Zone____ State_____

MAGNAVOX METROPOLITAN. Big Magnascope "60" screen. **$279⁵⁰**
Matching table, $20.

MAGNAVOX MODULAR Big Magnascope "90" screen and 12½" tube.

$349⁵⁰

Can be used as a table model or can be correlated with Magnavox Radio-Phonograph as shown in top picture.

25

Illustrated above: 1940 Studebaker Champion Club Sedan $700 delivered at factory

STUDEBAKER BEATS ALL OTHER CARS
in America's greatest gas economy classic

STUDEBAKER CHAMPION 29.19 MILES PER GALLON

On January 4, Studebaker's three great 1940 cars finished 1-2-3 in the Gilmore-Yosemite Sweepstakes, defeating all other cars entered. Under American Automobile Assn. supervision, the Studebaker Champion averaged 29.19 miles per gallon, the Studebaker Commander 24.72 miles per gallon, the Studebaker President 23.40 miles per gallon. Each was a strictly stock car, equipped with Studebaker's low-extra-cost overdrive.

Enjoy this distinction and save 10% to 25% every mile
STUDEBAKER CHAMPION

YOUR selection of a Studebaker Champion is no speculation but a real thrift investment.

The 10% to 25% greater economy which Studebaker Champion owners enjoy means that you steadily save 10% to 25% on gas, not to mention your reduced upkeep cost.

Priced on a level with the 3 other large-selling lowest price cars

You save, too, on equipment, because there's no extra charge for such indispensables as this Studebaker Champion's planar independent suspension and finest hydraulic shock absorbers, nonslam rotary door latches, front-compartment hood lock, sealed-beam headlamps, steering wheel gear shift, foot-regulated hydraulic brakes, shockless variable-ratio steering.

Thousands of delighted owners say that no other lowest price car they've tried is so restful, sure-footed and steady, as this safe, easy-handling Champion.

See your local Studebaker dealer now and go for a revealing 10-mile drive. Learn how easy it is to become a proud Champion owner, with your present car as part payment, on C.I.T. terms.

PRICES BEGIN AT $660
for a Champion coupe delivered at the factory, subject to change without notice

Money-saving long life! Studebaker's 7,700 matchless master craftsmen build your Champion to stay in sound running condition for years.

Delightful riding comfort! Every road is velvet smooth, thanks to planar independent suspension and finest hydraulic shock absorbers.

26

Vintage Gilbert Electric Train Set

Price: $29.95 + $5.98 for 150 Watt Transformer

Description: 3/16 inch scale model Gilbert American Flyer Electric AC Train Set, the train and all the carriages are over 5ft long. Gilbert Company was an American toy company was best known for Erector Construction sets. Gilbert expanded from the 1930s to the late 1950s to become one of the largest toy companies in the world but following the death of its founder A.C. Gilbert in the early 60's the company lost its way with the American Flyer products sold to Lionel.

Portable Electric Phonograph

Price: $5.75

Description: Portable Electric Phonograph with 6 records of nursery rhymes included.

Walnut Finished Piano in Spinet Style

Price: $8.85

Description: Child's Walnut Finished Piano in Spinet Style 22 inches high, 19 inches wide and 13 inches deep.

Brightly Enameled Steel Truck

Price: $1.59

Description: Nearly 2 ft long brightly enameled rugged steel truck from 1940.

Table Style Zellophone - Old Toy Xylophone

Price: $1.98 cents

Description: Table Style Zellophone (Xylophone) includes Song Book, each note is numbered 1 to 12 and the song book instructs the child on the number note to strike with small mallet.

World War II Model Plane Kits

Price: $1.00 for all five

Description Five World War II model plane kits cut them out and put them together, models include Curtiss Warhawk P-40, North American Mustang P-51 and the Bell Airacobra P-39 from the U.S. Air Force and the Hawker Typhoon and the Supermarine Spitfire from the British Airforce.

World War II Rose O'Neill Kewpie Doll

Price: $2.59

Description Kewpie dolls were based on illustrations by Rose O'Neill that appeared in Ladies' Home Journal in 1909; they were extremely popular from 1912 to the mid 1930's. They are still sold today based on her original illustrations.

AMERICAN BIRTHS OF 1940

Jack William Nicklaus was born January 21, 1940 and grew up in Columbus, Ohio. His nickname was The Golden Bear. He is an American retired professional golfer. Many believe him to be the greatest golfer of all time. Over a quarter-century, he won a record 18 major championships, three more than Tiger Woods. Nicklaus focused on the major championships—Masters Tournament, U.S. Open, Open Championship and PGA Championship—and played a selective schedule of regular PGA Tour events. He competed in 164 major tournaments, more than any other player, and finished with 73 PGA Tour victories, more than anyone except Sam Snead (82) and Woods (81).

Today Jack Nicklaus heads one of the world's largest golf course design companies. Among his courses is Harbor Town Golf Links. He is a member of the American Society of Golf Course Architects. Jack Nicklaus runs an event on the PGA Tour, the Memorial Tournament.

James Oliver Cromwell was born January 27, 1940 and is an American actor. James Cromwell was born in Los Angeles, California, and raised in Manhattan, New York. Cromwell's first television performance was in a 1974 episode of The Rockford Files playing Terry, a tennis instructor. A few weeks later, he began a recurring role as Stretch Cunningham on All in the Family. He had starring roles in the 1990s critically acclaimed films Babe (1995), The People vs. Larry Flynt (1996), The Education of Little Tree (1997), L.A. Confidential (1997), The Green Mile (1999), and Snow Falling on Cedars (1999). Cromwell has had additional successes on television throughout his career. His role as newspaper tycoon William Randolph Hearst in the television film RKO 281 earned him an Emmy Award nomination for Outstanding Supporting Actor in a Television Movie. The following year, he received his second Emmy Award nomination for playing Bishop Lionel Stewart on the NBC medical drama series ER. In 2018, he appeared in HBO's Succession, and Showtime's Counterpart.

Gene Francis Alan Pitney was born February 17, 1940 and sadly passed away April 5, 2006. He was an American singer-songwriter, musician, and sound engineer. Pitney was born in Hartford, Connecticut. He grew up in Rockville, now part of Vernon, Connecticut. Pitney scored his first chart single, which made the Top 40, the self-penned "(I Wanna) Love My Life Away," on which he played several instruments and multi-tracked the vocals. Pitney is also remembered for the Burt Bacharach–Hal David song "(The Man Who Shot) Liberty Valance", which peaked at No. 4 in 1962. Though it shares a title with the John Wayne western, the song was not used in the film because of a publishing dispute. That same year "Only Love Can Break a Heart" became his highest charting song in the US at No. 2, followed in December by "Half Heaven, Half Heartache", this reached No. 12 on the Billboard chart. His popularity in the UK market was ensured by the breakthrough success of "Twenty Four Hours from Tulsa," a Bacharach and David song, which peaked at No. 5 in Britain at the start of 1964.

William "Smokey" Robinson Jr. was born February 19, 1940 and is an American singer, songwriter, record producer, and former record executive. He was born and raised in Detroit Michigan. William Robinson was the founder and front man of the Motown vocal group the Miracles, for which he was also chief songwriter and producer. Robinson led the group from its 1955 origins as "the Five Chimes" until 1972, when he announced a retirement from the group to focus on his role as Motown's vice president. In August 1957, Robinson and the Miracles met songwriter Berry Gordy after a failed audition for Brunswick Records. Berry Gordy formed Tamla Records which was later reincorporated as Motown. The Miracles became one of the first acts signed to the label, although they had actually been with Gordy since before the formation of Motown Records. Between 1962 and 1966, Robinson was also one of the major songwriters and producers for Motown, penning many hit singles. After a year of retirement, Robinson announced his comeback with the release of the eponymous Smokey album, in 1973.

Peter Henry Fonda was born February 23, 1940 and passed away August 16, 2019 and was an American actor, director, and screenwriter. He was born in New York City. Fonda began guest starring on television shows like Naked City, The New Breed, Wagon Train, and The Defenders. Fonda's first film came when producer Ross Hunter was looking for a new male actor to romance Sandra Dee in Tammy and the Doctor (1963). He was cast in the role, in what was a minor hit. By the mid-1960s, Fonda was not a conventional "leading man" in Hollywood. As Playboy magazine reported, Fonda had established a "solid reputation as a dropout". He had become outwardly nonconformist and grew his hair long and took LSD regularly, alienating the "establishment" film industry. Fonda produced, co-wrote and starred in Easy Rider (1969), directed by Dennis Hopper. Easy Rider is about two long-haired bikers traveling through the southwestern and southern United States where they encounter intolerance and violence.

Mario Gabriele Andretti was born February 28, 1940 is an Italian-born American former racing driver, one of the most successful Americans in the history of the sport. He is one of only two drivers to have won races in Formula One, Indy Car, World Sports car Championship, and NASCAR (the other being Dan Gurney). During his career, Andretti won the 1978 Formula One World Championship, four Indy Car titles and IROC VI. To date, he remains the only driver ever to win the Indianapolis 500 (1969), Daytona 500 (1967) and the Formula One World Championship, and, along with Juan Pablo Montoya, the only driver to have won a race in the NASCAR Cup Series, Formula One, and an Indianapolis 500. No American has won a Formula One race since Andretti's victory at the 1978 Dutch Grand Prix. Andretti had 109 career wins on major circuits. Andretti had a long career in racing. He was the only person to be named United States Driver of the Year in three decades (1967, 1978, and 1984). He was also one of only three drivers to have won major races on road courses, paved ovals, and dirt tracks in one season.

Carlos Ray "Chuck" Norris was born March 10, 1940 is an American martial artist, actor, film producer and screenwriter. He was born in Ryan, Oklahoma and now resides in Texas. He joined the United States Air Force as an Air Policeman (AP) in 1958 and was sent to Osan Air Base, South Korea. It was there that Norris acquired the nickname Chuck and began his training in Tang Soo Do (tangsudo), an interest that led to black belts in that art and the founding of the Chun Kuk Do ("Universal Way") form. When he returned to the United States, he continued to serve as an AP at March Air Force Base in California. He won many martial arts championships and later founded his own school of fighting named Chun Kuk Do. Norris is a black belt in Tang Soo Do, Brazilian jiu jitsu and Judo. In 1969, Norris made his acting debut in the Dean Martin film The Wrecking Crew. In 1972, he acted as Bruce Lee's nemesis in the widely acclaimed martial arts movie Way of the Dragon. In 1984, Norris starred in Missing in Action, the first of a series of POW rescue fantasies themed around the Vietnam War POW.

James Edmund Caan born March 26, 1940 and is an American actor. James was born in the Bronx, New York and now lives in Beverley Hills, California. Caan's first television appearance was in an episode of Naked City. His first substantial film role was as a punk hoodlum in the 1964 thriller Lady in a Cage, which starred Olivia de Havilland, who praised Caan's performance. In 1972 Coppola cast him as the short-tempered Sonny Corleone in The Godfather. Originally, Caan was cast as Michael Corleone (Sonny's youngest brother). Caan reprised his role as Sonny Corleone for a flashback scene in The Godfather Part II (1974). Caan was one of many stars in the war film A Bridge Too Far (1977). From 1982 to 1987, Caan suffered from depression over his sister's death from leukemia, a growing problem with cocaine, and what he described as "Hollywood burnout," and did not act in any films. Caan returned to acting in 1987, when Coppola cast him as an army platoon sergeant for the 3rd US Infantry Regiment ("The Old Guard") in Gardens of Stone.

John Joseph Pavlick born April 8, 1940 – April 25, 2019 was an American professional basketball player. He was born in Martins Ferry, Ohio. He competed for 16 seasons with the Boston Celtics, winning eight NBA championships, four of them coming in his first four seasons with the team. Pavlick is the Celtics' all-time leader in points, scoring 26,395 points (20.8 points per game, 16th all-time in points scored in the NBA), and playing in 1,270 games (30th all-time). He became the first player to score 1,000 points in 16 consecutive seasons, with his best season coming during the 1970–71 season when he averaged 28.9 points per game. Pavlick was shrewd with his money during his playing career, and he invested much of his money in the Wendy's fast food chain during its formative years. The success of his investments left Pavlick with a comfortable income after retirement and he never had to work for a conventional salary again. He had no desire to coach; instead, he served as a corporate speaker. Pavlick had Parkinson's disease during his last years. He died on April 25, 2019, in Jupiter, Florida, seventeen days after his 79th birthday. The No. 17 was forever synonymous with Pavlick.

Nancy Patricia Pelosi born March 26, 1940 is an American Democratic Party politician serving as Speaker of the United States House of Representatives since January 2019, the only woman to have done so. First elected to Congress in 1987, she is the highest-ranking elected woman in United States history. As Speaker of the House, she is second in the presidential line of succession, immediately after the vice president. Nancy Pelosi was born in Baltimore to an Italian-American family. She was elected as a Democratic National Committee member from California, a position she would hold until 1996. Pelosi supported her long-time friend, John Murtha of Pennsylvania, for the position of House majority leader, the second-ranking post in the House Democratic caucus. In February 2018, Pelosi broke the record for longest speech in the House of Representatives when she spent more than eight hours. At the start of the 116th Congress, Pelosi thwarted President Trump's attempts to use the 2018–19 federal government shutdowns which she called a "hostage-taking" of civil servants.

Herbert Jeffrey Hancock born April 12, 1940 is an American pianist, keyboardist, bandleader, composer and actor and was born in Chicago, Illinois. Hancock received considerable attention when, in May 1963, he joined Davis's Second Great Quintet. Davis personally sought out Hancock, whom he saw as one of the most promising talents in jazz. While in Davis's band, Hancock also found time to record dozens of sessions for the Blue Note label, both under his own name and as a sideman with other musicians. Hancock also recorded several less-well-known but still critically acclaimed albums with larger ensembles – My Point of View (1963), Speak Like a Child (1968) and The Prisoner (1969). Hancock left Blue Note in 1969, signing with Warner Bros. Records. Hancock's three records released in 1971–73 later became known as the "Mwandishi" albums, so-called after a Swahili name Hancock sometimes used during this era. The year 2005 saw the release of a duet album called Possibilities. In 2006 Sony BMG Music Entertainment released the two-disc retrospective The Essential Herbie Hancock.

Alfredo James Pacino born April 25, 1940 known professionally as Al Pacino is an American actor and filmmaker. Al Pacino was born in East Harlem, New York City, to Italian American parents Salvatore and Rose Pacino. In his teenage years, Pacino was known as "Sonny" to his friends. He had ambitions to become a baseball player and was also nicknamed "The Actor". After four years at HB Studio, Pacino successfully auditioned for the Actors Studio. The Actors Studio is a membership organization of professional actors, theater directors, and playwrights in the Hell's Kitchen neighborhood of Manhattan. Pacino studied "method acting" under acting coach Lee Strasberg, who appeared with Pacino in the films The Godfather Part II and in ...And Justice for All. In 1973, Pacino co-starred in Scarecrow, with Gene Hackman, and won the Palme d'Or at the Cannes Film Festival. That same year, Pacino was nominated for an Academy Award for Best Actor after starring in Serpico. Pacino starred alongside Brad Pitt and Leonardo DiCaprio in Quentin Tarantino's comedy-drama Once Upon a Time in Hollywood, which was released on July 26, 2019.

Eric Hilliard Nelson born May 8, 1940 and passed away December 31, 1985 aged 45. He was known professionally as Ricky Nelson, was an American pop star, musician, and singer-songwriter. In 1957 he began a long and successful career as a popular recording artist. As one of the top "teen idols" of the 1950s. His fame led to a motion picture role co-starring alongside John Wayne and Dean Martin in Howard Hawk's western feature film Rio Bravo (1959). He placed 53 songs on the Billboard Hot 100, and its predecessors, between 1957 and 1973, including "Poor Little Fool" in 1958, which was the first #1 song on Billboard magazine. He recorded 19 additional Top 10 hits and was inducted into the Rock and Roll Hall of Fame on January 21, 1987. In 1996 Nelson was ranked #49 on TV Guide's 50 Greatest TV Stars of All Time. In the mid-1960s, Nelson began to move towards country music, becoming a pioneer in the country-rock genre. He was one of the early influences of the so-called "California Sound".

Nancy Sandra Sinatra born June 8, 1940 is an American singer and actress and grew up in Jersey City, New Jersey. In the late 1950s, Sinatra began to study music, dancing, and voice at the University of California, Los Angeles. She dropped out after a year, and made her professional debut in 1960 on her father's television special, The Frank Sinatra Timex Show: Welcome Home Elvis, celebrating the return of Elvis Presley from Europe following his discharge from service in the U.S. Army. Sinatra was signed to her father's label, Reprise Records, in 1961. Her first single, "Cuff Links and a Tie Clip", went largely unnoticed. Sinatra made her mark on the American (and British) music scene in early 1966 with "These Boots Are Made for Walkin'." A run of chart singles followed, including the two 1966 Top 10 hits "How Does That Grab You, Darlin'?" (U.S. No.7) and "Sugar Town" (U.S. No.5). At 54, Sinatra posed for Playboy in the May 1995 issue and made appearances on TV shows to promote her album One More Time. Sinatra received her own star on the Hollywood Walk of Fame on May 11, 2006.

Ramón Gerardo Antonio Estévez born August 3, 1940 and known professionally as Martin Sheen. Martin was born in Dayton, Ohio and is an American actor. Sheen was greatly influenced by the actor James Dean. During the 1960s and early 1970s, Sheen honed his skills as a guest star on a number of popular television series, including Insight (1960's-1980's), My Three Sons (1964), Flipper (1967), The F.B.I. (1968), Mission: Impossible (1969) and Hawaii Five-O (1970) to name but a few. In the spring of 1989, Sheen was named honorary mayor of Malibu, California. He promptly marked his appointment with a decree proclaiming the area "a nuclear-free zone, a sanctuary for aliens and the homeless, and a protected environment for all life, wild and tame". Sheen received six Emmy Award nominations for Outstanding Lead Actor in a Drama Series for his performance on The West Wing, for which he won a Golden Globe Award for Best Performance by an Actor in TV-Drama, as well as two SAG Awards for Outstanding Performance by a Male Actor in a Drama Series.

Raquel Welch born Jo Raquel Tejada; September 5, 1940 is an American actress and singer and grew up in Chicago, Illinois. Seeking an acting career, Welch entered San Diego State College on a theater arts scholarship in 1958. She got a job as a weather forecaster at KFMB, a local San Diego television station. She was cast in small roles in two films, A House Is Not a Home (1964) and the musical Roustabout (1964), an Elvis Presley film. She also landed small roles on the television series Bewitched, McHale's Navy and The Virginian and appeared on the weekly variety series The Hollywood Palace as a billboard girl and presenter. In 1968, Welch appeared with Frank Sinatra in the detective film Lady in Cement, a sequel to the film Tony Rome (1967). Welch's most controversial role came in Myra Breckinridge (1970). She took the role as the film's transsexual heroine in an attempt to be taken seriously as an actress, but the movie was a failure. In 1974, Welch won a Golden Globe Award for Best Motion Picture Actress in a Musical or Comedy for The Three Musketeers.

oe Jackson Gibbs born November 25, 1940 and is a retired American football oach, NASCAR Cup Series and NASCAR Xfinity Series team owner, and former JHRA team owner. Gibbs constructed what Steve Sabol has called, "The most diverse dynasty in NFL history", building championship teams from players who had mediocre to average performance while playing for other NFL teams. During his first stint in the National Football League, he led the Redskins to eight playoff appearances, four NFC Championship titles, and three Super Bowl titles over 12 seasons. Gibbs is the only head coach to have won Super Bowls with three different starting quarterbacks. After retiring at the end of the 1992 season, he switched focus to NASCAR team Joe Gibbs Racing, which has won four NASCAR Cup Series championships under his ownership. On January 7, 2004, Gibbs came out of retirement to rejoin the Redskins as head coach and team president, signing a five-year, $28.5 million contract. On January 8, 2008, Gibbs announced his final retirement from coaching.

Lee Jun-fan born November 27, 1940 and passed away July 20, 1973. He was known professionally as Bruce Lee was a Hong Kong-American actor, director, martial artist, martial arts instructor, and philosopher. He was born in San Francisco, California. He was the founder of Jeet Kune Do, a hybrid martial arts philosophy drawing from different combat disciplines that is often credited with paving the way for modern mixed martial arts (MMA). He is noted for his roles in five feature-length martial arts films in the early 1970s: Lo Wei's The Big Boss (1971) and Fist of Fury (1972); Golden Harvest's Way of the Dragon (1972), directed and written by Lee; Golden Harvest and Warner Brothers' Enter the Dragon (1973) and The Game of Death (1978). On May 10, 1973, Lee collapsed during an automated dialogue replacement session for Enter the Dragon at Golden Harvest in Hong Kong. Suffering from seizures and headaches, Lee's body is buried in Lake View Cemetery in Seattle. Pallbearers at Lee's funeral on July 25, 1973, included Taky Kimura, Steve McQueen, James Coburn, Chuck Norris, George Lazenby, Dan Inosanto, Peter Chin, and Lee's brother Robert.

Richard Franklin Lennox Thomas Pryor born December 1, 1940 and sadly passed away December 10, 2005. He was an American stand-up comedian and actor. Richard was born in Peoria, Illinois. Pryor served in the U.S. Army from 1958 to 1960, but spent virtually the entire stint in an army prison. Pryor was incarcerated for an incident that occurred while he was stationed in West Germany. Angered that a white soldier was overly amused at the racially charged scenes of Douglas Sirk's film Imitation of Life, Pryor and several other black soldiers beat and stabbed him, although not fatally. In 1983 Pryor signed a five-year contract with Columbia Pictures for $40 million and he started his own production company, Indigo Productions. Softer, more formulaic films followed, including Superman III (1983), which earned Pryor $4 million; Brewster's Millions (1985), Moving (1988), and See No Evil, Hear No Evil (1989). On December 10, 2005, nine days after his 65th birthday, Pryor suffered a heart attack in Los Angeles.

Marie Dionne Warwick born December 12, 1940 is a six-time Grammy Award-winning singer, actress, television host, and former United Nations Global Ambassador for the Food and Agriculture Organization and United States Ambassador of Health. She was born in Orange, New Jersey. In November 1962, Scepter Records released her first solo single, "Don't Make Me Over". Warwick weathered the British Invasion better than most American artists. Her biggest UK hits were "Walk On By" and "Do You Know the Way to San Jose?" In the UK, a number of Bacharach-David-Warwick songs were recorded by British singers Cilla Black, Sandie Shaw and Dusty Springfield, most notably Black's "Anyone Who Had a Heart" which went to No. 1 in the UK. In January 1980, while under contract to Arista Records, Warwick hosted a two-hour TV special called Solid Gold '79. This was adapted into the weekly one-hour show Solid Gold, which she hosted throughout 1980 and 1981 and again in 1985–86. She is one of the most-charted female vocalists of all time, with 56 of her singles making the Billboard Hot 100 between 1962 and 1998, and 80 singles.

Frank Vincent Zappa born December 21, 1940 and passed away December 4, 1993. He was an American multi-instrumentalist musician, composer, and bandleader. His work is characterized by nonconformity, free-form improvisation, sound experiments, musical virtuosity, and satire of American culture. In a career spanning more than 30 years, Zappa composed rock, pop, jazz, jazz fusion, orchestral and musique concrète works, and produced almost all of the 60-plus albums that he released with his band the Mothers of Invention and as a solo artist. Zappa also directed feature-length films and music videos, and designed album covers. He is considered one of the most innovative and stylistically diverse rock musicians of his era. Zappa died from prostate cancer on December 4, 1993, 17 days before his 53rd birthday at his home with his wife and children by his side. At a private ceremony the following day, his body was buried in a grave at the Westwood Village Memorial Park Cemetery, in Los Angeles. The grave is unmarked. On December 6, his family publicly announced that "Composer Frank Zappa left for his final tour just before 6:00 pm on Saturday".

SPORTING EVENTS 1940

1940 World Series

he 1940 World Series matched the Cincinnati Reds against the Detroit Tigers, the Reds winning a closely
ontested seven-game series for their second championship 21 years after their scandal-tainted victory in 1919.
his would be the Reds' last World Series championship for 35 years despite appearances in 1961, 1970, and
972. Meanwhile, Bill Klem worked the last of his record 18 World Series as an umpire.

NL Cincinnati Reds (4) vs. AL Detroit Tigers (3)

Game	Date	Score	Location	Time	Attendance
1	October 2	**Detroit Tigers** – 7, Cincinnati Reds – 2	Crosley Field	2:09	31,793
2	October 3	Detroit Tigers – 3, **Cincinnati Reds** – 5	Crosley Field	1:54	30,640
3	October 4	Cincinnati Reds – 4, **Detroit Tigers** – 7	Briggs Stadium	2:08	52,877
4	October 5	**Cincinnati Reds** – 5, Detroit Tigers – 2	Briggs Stadium	2:06	54,093
5	October 6	Cincinnati Reds – 0, **Detroit Tigers** – 8	Briggs Stadium	2:26	55,189
6	October 7	Detroit Tigers – 0, **Cincinnati Reds** – 4	Crosley Field	2:01	30,481
7	October 8	Detroit Tigers – 1, **Cincinnati Reds** – 2	Crosley Field	1:47	26,854

1940 NBL Champion

Akron Firestone Non-Skids - Champions 1940

The Akron Firestone Non-Skids were an American professional basketball team based in Akron, Ohio. The team was one of the thirteen founding members of the National Basketball League (NBL), which formed in 1937. The team was named for the Firestone Tire and Rubber Company, which was headquartered in Akron.

The team was founded by Firestone as an amateur industrial team. Like other industrial teams of the era, the players were company employees with year-round jobs who were not paid for basketball but owed their jobs to their basketball skills. The Non-Skids first competed professionally in the 1932–33 National Basketball League and defeated the Indianapolis Kautskys in the championship game. In 1935, the Non-Skids joined the Midwest Basketball Conference. In 1937, Firestone, General Electric, and Goodyear created the National Basketball League from company-sponsored teams and independent teams. The Non-Skids were NBL champions in 1939 and 1940, defeating the Oshkosh All-Stars both years in the Finals. Following the 1940–1941 season, the Akron Firestone Non-Skids disbanded, leaving the Akron Goodyear Wingfoot's as the only NBL team representing Akron.

Golf 1940 U.S. Open

William Lawson Little Jr. was an American professional golfer who also had a distinguished amateur career.

Little was born in Newport, Rhode Island, and lived much of his early life in the San Francisco area, where his father was a senior military officer. Little was one of the most dominant amateur players in the history of the sport, capturing both the British Amateur and the U.S. Amateur, and then regarded as major championships, consecutively in 1934 and 1935. He remains the only player to have won both titles in the same year more than once. Little's winning margin of 14 and 13 in the 1934 British final remains the record for dominance. Bob Dickson, Harold Hilton and Bobby Jones are the only other golfers to have won the two titles in the same year.

Little turned professional in April 1936, and he won eight times on the PGA Tour including one professional major, the 1940 U.S. Open. This tally was considered somewhat disappointing; he was said to have lost interest in golf during World War II, when the major championships were cancelled, and to have focused his attention more on the stock market. He carried up to 26 clubs in his bag, and this prompted the United States Golf Association to introduce the 14-club limit in 1938.

Little died in Monterey, California in 1968. He was inducted into the World Golf Hall of Fame in 1980.

He's The 1940 Open Golf Champion

Scorecard

Hole	1	2	3	4	5	6	7	8	9	10	11	12	13	14	15	16	17	18
Par	4	4	3	4	4	5	3	4	5	4	3	4	5	4	4	5	3	4
Little	E	−1	−1	−1	−2	−2	−2	−2	−2	−2	−2	−1	−1	−1	−2	−3	−2	−2
Sarazen	+1	+1	+1	+1	+2	E	+1	+1	+1	+1	E	E	+1	E	E	E	+1	+1

	Eagle		Birdie		Bogey	

Kentucky Derby Winner 1940

GALLAHADION

In the 1940 Kentucky Derby, Edward R. Bradley's colt Bimelech, the 1939 U.S. 2-Year-Old Champion, was the overwhelming favorite, bet down to 40¢ on the dollar. Mioland, owned by Charles S. Howard of Seabiscuit fame, was a very distant second choice at more than 6:1 odds. Given almost no chance, Gallahadion was sent off as a 36:1 longshot but under jockey Carroll Bierman scored an upset over Bimelech. For owner Ethel V. Mars, whom the May 9, 1940 Centralia Illinois Evening Sentinel reported had spent more than $500,000 buying horses since 1935 with the eye to winning the Derby. Gallahadion was her eighth horse to run in the Derby in the past six years. Previously, Mrs. Mars' best results came in 1935 and 1937 when her horses finished third. A severe cold kept her at home and she was not at Churchill Downs to see her horse capture the one race she had wanted to win most of all. In the second and third legs of the U.S. Triple Crown, Bimelech won both races. Gallahadion finished third in the Preakness Stakes, then found the extra distance in the 1½ mile Belmont Stakes too much and was unplaced.

Preakness Stakes and Belmont Stakes Winner 1940

BIMELECH

Bimelech was a champion Thoroughbred racehorse who won two Triple Crown races and was a Champion at both age two and three. Bimelech was undefeated as a two-year-old, winning his first over maidens at Suffolk Downs by three lengths. In his next race, an allowance at Empire City, he wired the field. Bimelech's first stakes race was at Saratoga Race Course, where he defeated Briar Sharp and Andy K. in the Saratoga Special Stakes. He then went on to win the Hopeful Stakes by a neck. He ended his first season with a length and a half victory in the Belmont Futurity Stakes and a four length win in the Pimlico Futurity. Bimelech was named American Champion Two-Year-Old Colt. He was also the Experimental Free Handicap Highweight at 130 pounds, a prodigious weight for a young horse.

He became the favorite to win the 1940 Kentucky Derby; his winterbook odds of three to one were the lowest odds ever quoted for a Derby favorite up to that time.

In his first race as a three-year-old, Bimelech took the Blue Grass Stakes by two and a half lengths. He then won the Derby Trial Stakes, beating a colt from Milky Way Farm Stable called Gallahadion.

Still undefeated, Bimelech was the overwhelming choice for the Derby, which had had its purse raised to $75,000 added. It was his third start in 8 days. At six to one, Charles S. Howard's Mioland was the bettor's second choice. (Howard owned and raced the famous Seabiscuit.) Gallahadion was thirty-five to one.

In the Derby, Bimelech drifted farther and farther out from the rail and ran wide the entire race. The longer distance left him exhausted in the last few furlongs. Gallahadion passed him in the final furlong. Bimelech's jockey, Fred Smith, took the blame for the loss.

A short time later, Bimelech beat Gallahadion in the Preakness. He ran second in the Withers Stakes, but records indicate this was due to poor preparation. So after the Withers, Bimelech went into heavy training), and won the Belmont Stakes. He struggled to win his next race, and it was discovered he was racing with an injured foot, which ended his racing that year. He took that year's honor of American Champion Three-Year-Old Male Horse.

Stanley Cup 1940

he New York Rangers are a professional ice hockey team ased in New York City. They are members of the Metropolitan Division of the Eastern Conference of the ational Hockey League (NHL).

ounded in 1926 by Tex Rickard, the Rangers are one of the riginal Six teams that competed in the NHL before its 1967 xpansion, along with the Boston Bruins, Chicago lackhawks, Detroit Red Wings, Montreal Canadians and oronto Maple Leafs. The team attained success early on nder the guidance of Lester Patrick, who coached a vibrant eam containing Frank Boucher, Murray Murdoch, and Bun nd Bill Cook to Stanley Cup glory in 1928, making them the rst NHL franchise in the United States to win the trophy. he team would then go onto win two additional Stanley ups in 1933 and 1940.

NEW YORK RANGERS 1939–1940

he 1940 Stanley Cup finals commenced in Madison Square Garden in New York. The first two games went to the angers. In Game 1, the Rangers needed overtime to gain a 1–0 series lead, but they won game two more easily ith a 6–2 victory. The series then shifted to Toronto, where the Maple Leafs won the next two games, tying the eries at two games apiece. In Games 5 and 6, the Rangers won in overtime, taking the series four games to two earn their third Stanley Cup.

US Open Men's singles tennis champion 1940

William Donald McNeill In 1939, McNeill became the second American to win the French Championships singles title (after Don Budge) when he defeated compatriot Bobby Riggs in the final in straight sets.

Afterwards he played at Wimbledon, the only time he participated, and lost to Franjo Kukuljevic in the second round of the singles, reached the third round in the doubles and the quarterfinal in the mixed doubles.

He went on to win the All England Plate, a tennis competition held at the Wimbledon Championships which consisted of players who were defeated in the first or second rounds of the singles competition.

In June 1940 McNeill beat Bobby Riggs to win the singles title at the U.S. Men's Clay Court Championships in Chicago.

US Open Ladies singles tennis champion 1940

Alice Marble. At the U.S. Championships, Marble won the singles title in 1936 and from 1938 to 1940, the women's doubles title with Sarah Palfrey Cooke from 1937 to 1940, and the mixed doubles title with Gene Mako in 1936, Don Budge in 1938, Harry Hopman in 1939, and Bobby Riggs in 1940.

At Wimbledon, Marble won the singles title in 1939; the women's doubles title with Cooke in 1938 and 1939, and the mixed doubles title with Budge in 1937 and 1938 as well as the mixed doubles title with Riggs in 1939.

In Wightman Cup team competition, Marble lost only one singles and one doubles match in the years she competed (1933, 1937–39).

According to A. Wallis Myers and John Olliff of The Daily Telegraph and the Daily Mail, Marble was ranked in the world top ten from 1936 to 1939 (no rankings issued 1940–45), reaching a career high in those rankings of world No. 1 in 1939. Marble was included in the year-end top ten rankings issued by the United States Lawn Tennis Association in 1932–33 and 1936–40. She was the top-ranked U.S. player from 1936 to 1940.

Alice Marble was the Associated Press Athlete of the Year in 1939 and 1940.
After capping a stellar amateur career in 1940, Marble turned professional and earned more than $100,000, travelling around playing exhibition tournaments

1940 AAA Championship Car season

The 1940 AAA Championship Car season consisted of three races, beginning in Speedway, Indiana on May 30 and concluding in Syracuse, New York on September 2. There was also one non-championship event in Langhorne, Pennsylvania. The AAA National Champion was Rex Mays and the Indianapolis 500 winner was Wilbur Shaw.

#	Driver	Team	Points
1	Rex Mays	Bowes Seal Fast	1225
2	Wilbur Shaw	Boyle	1000
3	Mauri Rose	Elgin Piston Pin	675
4	Ted Horn	Ted Horn Engineering	625
5	Joel Thorne	Thorne Engineering	450

Rex Houston Mays, Jr. was a former AAA Championship Car race driver. He was a two-time AAA champion and won 8 points-scoring races. He made his Indianapolis 500 debut in 1934 and won the pole in 1935, 1936, and again in 1940 and finished second, he returned the next year and finished second again. Mays won the AAA National Championship in 1940 and 1941. However, World War II suspended racing until 1946, denying Mays of what likely would have been the peak of his career. After the war, Mays again won the Indy pole in 1948 but was knocked out by a mechanical problem.

He was killed at the age of 36 in a crash during the only Champ Car race held at Del Mar Fairgrounds race track in Del Mar, California in November 1949. In this accident, Mays swerved to miss a car that had crashed in front of him. His car went out of control and flipped, throwing Mays to the track surface, where he was hit by a trailing car.

Wilbur Shaw won the Indianapolis 500 race three times, in 1937, 1939 and 1940. Shaw was the second person to win the 500 three times, and the first to win it twice in a row. In the 1941 race, Shaw was injured when his car crashed; it was later discovered that a defective wheel had been placed on his car. During World War II, Shaw was hired by the tire manufacturer Firestone Tire and Rubber Company to test a synthetic rubber automobile tire at the Indianapolis Motor Speedway, which had been closed due to the war. He was dismayed at the dilapidated condition of the racetrack and quickly contacted then-owner Eddie Rickenbacker. When the United States entered World War II, ending racing at Indianapolis and elsewhere for the duration, Rickenbacker padlocked the gates and let the race course slowly begin to disintegrate. Shaw was killed in an airplane crash near Decatur, Indiana, on October 30, 1954, one day before his fifty-second birthday.

BOOKS PUBLISHED IN 1940

Native Son published March 1, 1940 is a novel written by the American author Richard Wright. It tells the story of 20-year-old Bigger Thomas, a black youth living in utter poverty in a poor area on Chicago's South Side in the 1930s.

While not apologizing for Bigger's crimes, Wright portrays a systemic inevitability behind them. Bigger's lawyer, Boris Max, makes the case that there is no escape from this destiny for his client or any other black American since they are the necessary product of the society that formed them and told them since birth who exactly they were supposed to be.

"No American Negro exists", James Baldwin once wrote, "who does not have his private Bigger Thomas living in his skull." Frantz Fanon discusses the feeling in his 1952 essay, L'expérience vécue du noir (The Fact of Blackness). "In the end", writes Fanon, "Bigger Thomas acts. To put an end to his tension, he acts, he responds to the world's anticipation." The book was a successful and ground-breaking best seller. However, it was also criticized by Baldwin and others as ultimately advancing Bigger as a stereotype, not a real character.

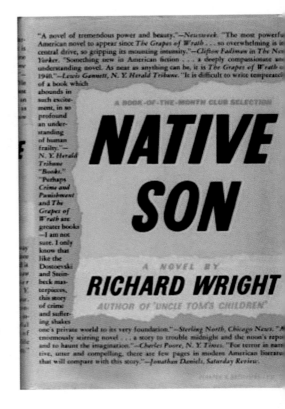

The Heart Is a Lonely Hunter (1940) is the debut novel by the American author Carson McCullers; she was 23 at the time of publication. It is about a deaf man named John Singer and the people he encounters in a 1930s mill town in the US state of Georgia.

The book begins with a focus on the relationship between two close friends, John Singer and Spiros Antonapoulos. The two are described as deaf-mutes who have lived together for several years. Antonapoulos becomes mentally ill, misbehaves, and despite attempts at intervention from Singer, is eventually put into an insane asylum away from town. Now alone, Singer moves into a new room.

The remainder of the narrative centers on the struggles of four of John Singer's acquaintances: Mick Kelly, a tomboyish girl who loves music and dreams of buying a piano; Jake Blount, an alcoholic labor agitator; Biff Brannon, the observant owner of a diner; and Dr. Benedict Mady Copeland, an idealistic black physician.

Four Quartets is a set of four poems written by T. S. Eliot that were published over a six-year period. The first poem, Burnt Norton, was published with a collection of his early works (1936's Collected Poems 1909–1935.) After a few years, Eliot composed the other three poems, East Coker, The Dry Salvages, and Little Gidding, which were written during World War II and the air-raids on Great Britain. They were first published as a series by Faber and Faber in Great Britain between 1940 and 1942 towards the end of Eliot's poetic career (East Coker in September 1940, Burnt Norton in February 1941, The Dry Salvages in September 1941 and Little Gidding in 1942.) The poems were not collected until Eliot's New York publisher printed them together in 1943.

Four Quartets are four interlinked meditations with the common theme being man's relationship with time, the universe, and the divine. In describing his understanding of the divine within the poems, Eliot blends his Anglo-Catholicism with mystical, philosophical and poetic works from both Eastern and Western religious and cultural traditions, with references to the Bhagavad-Gita and the Pre-Socratics as well as St. John of the Cross and Julian of Norwich.

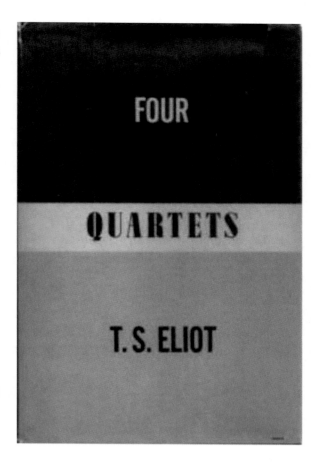

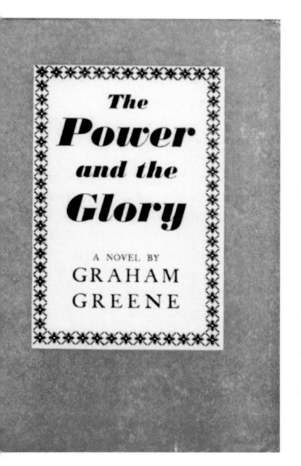

The Power and the Glory (1940) is a novel by British author Graham Greene. The title is an allusion to the doxology often recited at the end of the Lord's Prayer: "For thine is the kingdom, the power, and the glory, forever and ever, amen." It was initially published in the United States under the title The Labyrinthine Ways. Greene's novel tells the story of a renegade Roman Catholic 'whisky priest' (a term coined by Greene) living in the Mexican state of Tabasco in the 1930s, a time when the Mexican government was attempting to suppress the Catholic Church. That suppression had resulted in the Cristero War (1927-1929), so named for its Catholic combatants' slogan Viva Cristo Rey (long live Christ the King). In 1941, the novel received the Hawthornden Prize British literary award. In 2005, it was chosen by TIME magazine as one of the hundred best English-language novels since 1923. The main character is an unnamed 'whisky priest', who combines a great power for self-destruction with pitiful cravenness, an almost painful penitence, and a desperate quest for dignity. By the end, though, the priest "acquires a real holiness." The other principal character is a police lieutenant tasked with hunting down this priest. This Lieutenant — also unnamed but thought to be based upon Tomás Garrido Canabal — is a committed socialist who despises the Church.

Fanny by Gaslight is the best known novel of Michael Sadleir. Written in 1940 and filmed in 1944, it is a fictional exploration of prostitution in Victorian London. In 1981 it was turned into a four-part BBC television series Fanny by Gaslight with Chloe Salaman in the title role.

Fanny (Phyllis Calvert) finishes at boarding school in 1880 and returns to London, where she witnesses Lord Manderstoke (James Mason) fight and kill her supposed father. She soon learns that her family has run a brothel next door to her home and (on her mother's death) that he was not her real father. She goes to meet her real father – a respected politician – and falls in love with Harry Somerford (Stewart Granger), his advisor. Manderstoke continues to thwart her happiness.

Michael Sadleir's best known novel was Fanny by Gaslight (1940), a fictional exploration of prostitution in Victorian London. It was adapted under that name as a 1944 film. The 1947 novel Forlorn Sunset further explored the characters of the Victorian London underworld. His writings also include a biography of his father, published in 1949, and a privately published memoir of one of his sons, who was killed in World War II.

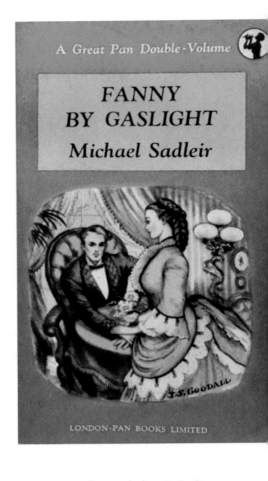

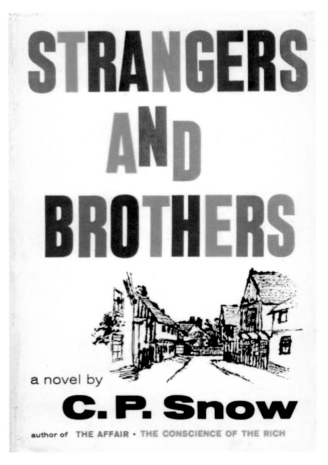

Strangers and Brothers is a series of novels by C. P. Snow, published between 1940 and 1970. They deal with – among other things – questions of political and personal integrity, and the mechanics of exercising power. All eleven novels in the series are narrated by the character Lewis Eliot. The series follows his life and career from humble beginnings in an English provincial town, to reasonably successful London lawyer, to Cambridge don, to wartime service in Whitehall, to senior civil servant and finally retirement. The New Men deals with the scientific community's involvement in (and reaction to) the development and deployment of nuclear weapons during the Second World War. The Conscience of the Rich concerns a wealthy, Anglo-Jewish merchant-banking family. Snow analyses the professional world, scrutinizing microscopic shifts of power within the enclosed settings of a Cambridge college, a Whitehall ministry, a law firm. For example, in the novels set in the Cambridge college a small, disparate group of men is typically required to reach a collective decision on an important subject. In The Masters, the dozen or so college members elect a new head by majority vote. In The Affair, a small group of dons sets out to correct a possible injustice: they must convince the rest of the college to re-open an investigation into scientific fraud.

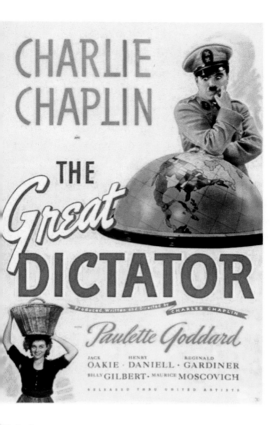

The Great Dictator. 20 years after the end of WWI, in which the nation of Tomainia was on the losing side, Adenoid Hynkel has risen to power as the ruthless dictator of the country. He believes in a pure Aryan state and the decimation of the Jews. This situation is unknown to a simple Jewish Tomainian barber who has been hospitalized since a WWI battle. Upon his release the barber, who had been suffering from memory loss about the war, is shown the new persecuted life of the Jews by many living in the Jewish ghetto, including a washerwoman named Hannah with whom he begins a relationship. The barber is ultimately spared such persecution by Commander Schultz, whom he saved in that WWI battle. The lives of all Jews in Tomainia are eventually spared with a policy shift by Hynkel himself, who is doing so for ulterior motives

Box Office
Budget:$2,000,000 (estimated)
Cumulative Worldwide Gross: $952,732

Run time is 2h 5mins

Trivia

Adolf Hitler banned the film in Germany and in all countries occupied by the Nazis. Curiosity got the best of him, and he had a print brought in through Portugal. History records that he screened it twice, in private, but history did not record his reaction to the film. Charles Chaplin said, "I'd give anything to know what he thought of it." For political reasons in Germany, the ban stayed after the end of WWII until 1958.

This film was financed entirely by Charles Chaplin himself, and it was his biggest box-office hit.

Released eleven years after the end of the silent era, this was Charles Chaplin's first all-talking, all-sound film.

According to documentaries on the making of the film, Charles Chaplin began to feel more uncomfortable lampooning Adolf Hitler the more he heard of Hitler's actions in Europe. Ultimately, the invasion of France inspired Chaplin to change the ending of his film to include his famous speech.

Goofs

(at around 30 mins) When the Jewish Barber has just returned to the Ghetto and is cleaning his windows, his white overcoat changes from buttoned to unbuttoned throughout the fight scene.

(at around 27 mins) When Hannah has tomatoes thrown at her by the soldiers, she has 3 prominent streaks of dirt on her right cheek as she cowers down to protect herself. When she gets up after the attack, the dirt is missing from her cheek.

(at around 30 mins) When the Jewish Barber cleans the word "Jew" off his shop window, a dotted line can be seen to mark where the W would be painted again for the next take.

The Shop Around The Corner. Alfred Kralik is the senior salesman in a long established Budapest gift shop, owned by the likeable and kindly Hugo Matuschek. Alfred has been there for 9 years and is very good at his job. One day a young woman, Klara Novak, comes into the shop looking for a job. They don't really have a position available but she impresses Mr. Matuschek with her skills and is taken on. Alfred and Klara don't get along very well but unbeknownst to either of them, they have been corresponding anonymously. On the day he is to meet her finally, Alfred is fired for reasons that are not clear to him. He has always gotten along well with Mr. Matuschek who it turn out, suspects him of having an affair with his wife. He's wrong of course but that evening, Alfred sees that Klara is the one he has been corresponding with. He's soon back in the shop as manager when Mr. Matuschek realizes his error but the question now is how he could possibly impress Klara without revealing who he is.

Box Office
Cumulative Worldwide Gross: $36,368

Run time 1h 29mins

Trivia
Soon after wrapping principal photography, Ernst Lubitsch talked to the New York Sun in January 1940. "It's not a big picture, just a quiet little story that seemed to have some charm. It didn't cost very much, for such a cast, under $500,000. It was made in twenty-eight days. I hope it has some charm."

To make sure his film was stripped of the glamour usually associated with him, Ernst Lubitsch went to such lengths as ordering that a dress Margaret Sullavan had purchased off the rack for $1.98 be left in the sun to bleach and altered to fit poorly.

James Stewart and Margaret Sullavan had known each other a long time before making this film. Both were in a summer stock company called the University Players. It was there that Stewart realized his potential as an actor, so he followed Sullavan and fellow player Henry Fonda to New York to begin an acting career in earnest.

Goofs
Before they leave the store room Alfred takes 5 boxes and Klara 4. In the next cut, suddenly Klara carries 5 boxes and Alfred has 4.

When Klara hurries out of the back room with her hat and coat she rushes past the rest of the employees as they enter the room in a group. Flora is the second-to-last person in the line and she is clearly inside the room before Klara runs past. In the next cut showing Klara hurrying through the store, Flora is the last person in line and is still in the doorway.

After dismissing his employees for the night, Mr. Matuschek sees Vadas leave the shop. As he watches him close the door, you can clearly hear off camera directions that sound like "turn" and "he's gone."

Rebecca. A young woman is in Monte Carlo, working as a ladies' companion, when she meets the recently-widowed, and very wealthy, Maxim De Winter. They fall in love and get married soon thereafter. The De Winters take up residence in Maxim's family estate, Mandalay. Mrs. De Winter finds it hard to fit in.

The presence of Maxim's deceased wife, Rebecca, seems to permeate through the house and Mrs. De Winter can't shake the feeling that she is constantly being compared to her and that she is an interloper.

Mrs. Danvers, Rebecca's personal maid, also takes care to make things as uncomfortable as possible for the new Mrs. De Winter. Mrs. De Winter has the constant fear that memories of Rebecca will drive her and Maxim apart. Over time, she grows to know more and more about Rebecca.

Box Office
Budget:$1,288,000 (estimated)
Cumulative Worldwide Gross: $72,275

Run time 2h 10mins.

Trivia

Because Sir Laurence Olivier wanted his then-girlfriend Vivien Leigh to play the lead role, he treated Joan Fontaine horribly. This shook Fontaine up quite a bit, so Sir Alfred Hitchcock decided to capitalize on this by telling her everyone on the set hated her, thus making her shy and uneasy, just what he wanted from her performance.

The first movie that Sir Alfred Hitchcock made in Hollywood, and the only one that won a Best Picture Oscar. Although it won Best Picture, the Best Director Award that year went to John Ford for The Grapes of Wrath (1940).

In order to maintain the dark atmosphere of the book, Sir Alfred Hitchcock insisted that this movie be shot in black and white.

Goofs

The word pamplemousse (French for grapefruit) is incorrectly spelled as 'pamplemouse' in the Princess Hotel Monte Carlo menu toward the beginning of the film.

When Mrs. Danvers draws open the draperies in Rebecca's room, she tugs very slightly at the draw cord causing the huge drapes to open several feet.

The large map on the courtroom wall is a map of the Americas. It is grossly implausible that such a map would be on the wall of an English courtroom.

The Grapes Of Wrath. The Joad clan, introduced to the world in John Steinbeck's iconic novel, is looking for a better life in California. After their drought-ridden farm is seized by the bank, the family -- led by just-paroled son Tom -- loads up a truck and heads West. On the road, beset by hardships, the Joads meet dozens of other families making the same trek and holding onto the same dream. Once in California, however, the Joads soon realize that the promised land isn't quite what they hoped.

Winner of two Oscars in 1941 for:

Best Actress in a Supporting Role	Jane Darwell
Best Director	John Ford

Nominated for:
Best Picture	
Best Actor in a Leading Role	Henry Fonda
Best Writing, Screenplay	Nunnally Johnson
Best Sound, Recording	Edmund H. Hansen
Best Film Editing	Robert L. Simpson

Run time 2h 9mins uncut

Trivia

Prior to filming, producer Darryl F. Zanuck sent undercover investigators out to the migrant camps to see if John Steinbeck had been exaggerating about the squalor and unfair treatment meted out there. He was horrified to discover that, if anything, Steinbeck had actually downplayed what went on in the camps.

John Steinbeck was particularly enamored with the performance of Henry Fonda as Tom Joad, feeling that he perfectly encapsulated everything he wanted to convey with this character. The two became good friends. Indeed Fonda did a reading at Steinbeck's funeral.

While filming the Joads' car traveling down the highway, John Ford wanted to add a shot showing the large number of caravans heading west, so the film's business manager stopped actual cars making the trek and paid the drivers five dollars to escort the Joads' jalopy for the cameras.

Goofs

One of the cars (License plate 263 with the silver bed springs sticking out the back) evacuating the Department of Agriculture camp site leaves the camp twice, once before the Joads pack up and once after.

In the beginning of the movie Grandma Joad is sitting at the table eating with a full set of teeth in her mouth. Later when they stop to buy the bread Pa Joad explains to the waitress that they need to soften the bread for Grandma to eat because she has no teeth.

Tom Joad's semi-retarded brother, Noah, vanishes after the swimming-in-the-river sequence. In the book, Noah believes he's a burden on the family and runs away. In the film, no explanation is given for his disappearance.

The Philadelphia Story. A Philadelphia socialite C.K. Dexter Haven as he's being tossed out of his palatial home by his wife, Tracy Lord. Adding insult to injury, Tracy breaks one of C.K.'s precious golf clubs. He gallantly responds by knocking her down on her million-dollar keester. A couple of years after the breakup, Tracy are about to marry George Kittridge, a wealthy stuffed shirt whose principal recommendation is that he's not a Philadelphia mainliner, as C.K. was. Still holding a torch for Tracy, C.K. is galvanized into action when he learns that Sidney Kidd, the publisher of Spy Magazine, plans to publish an exposé concerning Tracy's philandering father). To keep Kidd from spilling the beans, C.K. agrees to smuggle Spy reporter Macauley Connor and photographer Elizabeth Imbrie into the exclusive Lord-Kittridge wedding ceremony. How could C.K. have foreseen that Connor would fall in love with Tracy, thereby nearly lousing up the nuptials? As it turns out, of course, it is C.K. himself who pulls the louse-up, reclaiming Tracy as his bride.

Box Office
Gross USA: $404,524
Cumulative Worldwide Gross: $411,442

Run time 1h 52mins

Trivia

The film was shot in eight weeks, and required no retakes. During the scene where James Stewart hiccups when drunk, you can see Cary Grant looking down and grinning. Since the hiccup wasn't scripted, Grant was on the verge of breaking out laughing and had to compose himself quickly. Stewart (apparently spontaneously) thought of hiccupping in the drunken scene, without telling Grant. When he began hiccupping, Grant turned to Stewart saying, "Excuse me." The scene required only one take.

James Stewart never felt he deserved the Best Actor Oscar for his performance in this film, especially since he had initially felt miscast. He always maintained that Henry Fonda should have won instead for The Grapes of Wrath (1940), and that the award was probably "deferred payment for my work on Mr. Smith Goes to Washington (1939)."

Spencer Tracy turned down James Stewart's role because he was eager to make Dr. Jekyll and Mr. Hyde (1941).

Goofs

In the closing scene, a miscue by Grant and possible one by Hepburn, come off OK. Tracy opens a side door to announce to the guests that she and her fiancé "that was" have decided to call it a day. Dexter is standing behind her, and she says, "uh ... Dexter, what next?" He says "Three (sic) years ago I did you out of a wedding in this house by eloping to Maryland." She says to the guests, "Two years ago, uh, you were invited ..." She corrected the number of years which Grant clearly states wrongly - three, to two, but in catching and correcting his error, she got the rest of the line wrong.

As Connor and Tracy exit the library, the boom mic is reflected on the windshield of Tracy's car.

His Girl Friday. Four months after her resignation journalist Hildy Johnson returns to The Morning Post - just to tell her former boss and husband Walter Burns to stop bombarding her with telegrams because she won't come back to him, and anyway, she is going to marry insurance agent Bruce Baldwin the next day. When Walter learns that Hildy and Bruce are going to Albany already in two hours, he has to act very quickly. He immediately starts a series of clever schemes to get Bruce out of the way and Hildy back to journalism. He knows that Hildy cannot resist an enticing commission. Earl Williams is a confused man, who is going to be executed the following day; if not The Morning Post succeeds in convincing the governor to pardon him. Hildy sees the possibilities to get a scoop by interviewing Williams, and postpones her departure some hours. She gets more and more entangled in the case, and even helps Williams to hide, when he has run away from prison. Soon she and Walter work feverishly side by side, and her fiancé Bruce just annoys her.

Box Office
Gross USA: $296,000

Run time 1h 32mins

Trivia
Rosalind Russell thought, while shooting, that she didn't have as many good lines as Cary Grant had, so she hired an advertisement writer through her brother-in-law and had him write more clever lines for the dialog. Since Howard Hawks allowed for spontaneity and ad-libbing, he, and many of the cast and crew didn't notice it, but Grant knew she was up to something, leading him to greet her every morning: "What have you got today?"

One of the first films (preceded by "Stage Door" (1937)) to have characters talk over the lines of other characters, for a more realistic sound. Prior to this, movie characters completed their lines before the next lines were started.

To maintain the fast pace, Howard Hawks encouraged his cast to add dialogue and funny bits of business and step on each other's lines whenever possible.

Goofs
When Bruce Baldwin comes to the press room late in the movie, an electric fan and small shelf on the wall to the left of the door both completely disappear. Both have been there in all previous scenes and both reappear after this scene.

After Walter's check-up, he puts his tie back on. At first, the skinny (back) end of the tie is longer than the wide (front) end. In the next shot, the front is properly longer than the back. When he goes to put his coat on, the back is longer than the front again.

When Walter goes to take Hildy and Bruce to lunch, his hat jumps from his right hand to his left hand between shots.

Waterloo Bridge. At the start of WWII, General Roy Cronin, standing mid-span of Waterloo Bridge in London as he is set to go off to war in France, recalls that exact place in a time during WWI when he met by chance the love of his life, Myra Lester. Then, he was an Army Captain, she a member of a ballet troupe and school, their meeting during an air raid. He was set to return to the trenches in France the following day, by which time they knew that they were the ones for each other, they wanting to get married before his departure so that she could live with his supportive upper crust mother, Lady Margaret Cronin. But issues in their respective lives threatened a happily-ever-after for them. For him, it is the hazards of battle and the possibility that he would never make it back alive. For her, it was the ballet troupe's strict and uncompromising head, Madame Olga Kirowa, who expected all her ballerinas to focus solely on ballet which meant no personal life. In Myra possibly needing to choose between the troupe or Roy and something else, that something else was never a certainty.

Box Office
Cumulative Worldwide Gross: $31,111

Run time 1h 48mins

Trivia

The scene in which Myra and Roy dance to "Auld Lang Syne" was supposed to have dialogue, but nobody could come up with the right words. At about 3:00 in the morning before shooting the scene was to take place, Mervyn LeRoy, a veteran of silent films, realized that there shouldn't be any lines and that the images should speak for themselves. The result is the most celebrated scene of the film.

Released a few months after the German and Soviet invasion of Poland, and in the middle of the invasion of France and the Low Countries, this is likely the earliest Hollywood film to include the Second World War in its plot.

Rita Carlyle played (uncredited) the Old Woman on Bridge in BOTH Waterloo Bridge (1931) & Waterloo Bridge (1940). It was the woman who dropped her basket of potatoes and cabbage in the earlier version and the flower lady in the later version.

Goofs

Even though the story takes place during the pre-1920 World War I period, all of Myra's clothes and hairstyles are strictly in the up-to-the-minute 1940 fashion.

When Roy and Myra are coming out of the Underground station after the air raid near the beginning of the film a traffic light is clearly visible in the top right hand corner. There were no traffic lights in London until 1931.

The uniforms worn by the officers are more like US uniforms in cut and cloth than British. Roy's officer's hat is distinctly American in shape.

The Mortal Storm. On January 30, 1933 in a small village in southern Germany, Professor Roth celebrates his 60th birthday. It's also the day that Adolf Hitler becomes Chancellor of Germany. The professor is admired by his colleagues and students and much loved by his wife, stepsons Otto and Erich, and his daughter Freya. Otto, Erich and Freya's fiancé Fritz Marburg are all become avid Nazis and Professor Roth, who is a "non-Aryan", is soon sent to a concentration camp. Freya ends her engagement to Martin and she and her lifelong friend Martin Breitner soon fall in love. The oppressive regime forces Martin to flee to Austria and after the professor dies Freya and her mother try to flee but Freya is detained. Martin comes to her rescue but they must escape a Nazi patrol that is tracking them down.

Soundtracks
Close Up the Ranks
(1864) (uncredited)
Written by S.F. Cameron
Sung by bar patrons

Run time 1h 40mins

Trivia

Nazi leader Adolf Hitler banned this film from release in Germany because of its strong anti-Nazi sentiments. In addition, all MGM films from that point until the end of the war were also banned in Germany because the studio made this one.

When this movie was made, America was not part of World War II. Most of the heads of the major studios in Hollywood were for American involvement in the war. This movie is one of a number made during the late 1930s and early 1940s that represented this belief. These films include A Yank in the R.A.F. (1941), Man Hunt (1941), Foreign Correspondent (1940), Confessions of a Nazi Spy (1939) and Sergeant York (1941).

Although the resolution of the story hinges upon Martin & Freya escaping from Germany, and crossing the border into Austria, before the film was even made, Austria had already become under Nazi control, and so their troubles would not have ended there, by any means.

At the start of the movie, Prof. Roth (Frank Morgan) is experiencing his 60th birthday. In fact, when Frank Morgan filmed that scene he was closer to his 50th birthday and unfortunately did not live in real life to see his 60th.

Margaret Sullavan, Jimmy Stewart, and Frank Morgan all starred in The Shop Around the Corner (1940), which was released just six months before this movie.

Goofs

Although the story takes place in 1933, Margaret Sullavan's hairstyle and clothing are strictly in the 1940 mode.

Fantasia. An innovative and revolutionary animated classic from Walt Disney, combining Western classical music masterpieces with imaginative visuals, presented with Leopold Stokowski and the Philadelphia Orchestra. The eight animation sequences are colorful, impressive, free-flowing, abstract, and often surrealistic pieces. They include the most famous of all, Paul Dukas's "The Sorcerer's Apprentice" with Mickey Mouse as the title character battling brooms carrying endless buckets of water. Also included are J.S. Bach's "Toccata and Fugue in D Minor"; Tchaikovsky's "Nutcracker Suite"; dinosaurs and volcanoes in Stravinsky's "Rite of Spring"; the delightful "Dance of the Hours" by Ponchielli with dancing hippos, crocodiles, ostriches, and elephants; and Mussorgsky's darkly apocalyptic "Night on Bald Mountain."

Box Office
Budget:$2,280,000 (estimated)
Gross USA: $76,408,097
Cumulative Worldwide Gross: $76,411,401

Run time 2h 5mins uncut

Trivia

Walt Disney himself related the story of a chance meeting with Leopold Stokowski at Chasen's restaurant. They agreed to have dinner together. As they talked, Disney told of his plans to do "The Sorcerer's Apprentice" and other possible projects using classical music with animation. Disney said that he was stunned when Stokowski, then one of the two most famous conductors in the country (the other being Arturo Toscanini), responded by saying, "I would like to conduct that for you." It was an offer he couldn't pass up.

Even after more than 60 years after its release, Disney still receives complaints from parents claiming the "Night on Bald Mountain" sequence terrified their children.

The animators secretly modelled elements of the Sorcerer in "The Sorcerer's Apprentice" on their boss, Walt Disney. The raised eyebrow was regarded as a dead giveaway. They call the character Yen Sid, which is "Disney", spelled backwards.

Goofs

The creatures gathered at the dinosaur water hole include animal's exclusive to different time periods. Stegosaurs lived only in the Jurassic Period, Ceratopsians only in the Cretaceous and Dimetrodons only in the Permian. It is possible that this was not yet known in 1940.

When introducing the "Pastoral" sequence, Deems Taylor mixes Greek and Roman names of deities: Bacchus, Vulcan and Diana are Roman; Zeus, Iris and Morpheus are Greek. Apollo is the only one who's Greek and Roman equivalents have the same name.

Sea Hawk. Geoffrey Thorpe is an adventurous and dashing pirate, who feels that he should pirate the Spanish ships for the good of England. In one such battle, he overtakes a Spanish ship and when he comes aboard he finds Dona Maria, a beautiful Spanish royal. He is overwhelmed by her beauty, but she will have nothing to do with him because of his pirating ways (which include taking her prized jewels). To show his noble side, he surprises her by returning the jewels, and she begins to fall for him.

When the ship reaches England, Queen Elizabeth is outraged at the actions of Thorpe and demands that he quit pirating. Because he cannot do this, Thorpe is sent on a mission and in the process becomes a prisoner of the Spaniards. Meanwhile, Dona Maria pines for Thorpe and when he escapes he returns to England to uncover some deadly secrets. Exciting duels follow as Thorpe must expose the evil and win Dona Maria's heart.

Box Office
Budget:$1,700,000 (estimated)

Run time 2h 7mins

Trivia

Henry Daniell couldn't fence. The climactic duel had to be filmed using a double and skillful inter-cutting.

The scenes of Doña Maria's carriage traveling through the countryside were taken from David Copperfield (1935). The film had to be darkened to disguise the fact that the carriage depicted was clearly too modern for this film's Elizabethan setting.

The Panamian sequences were deliberately tinted in sepia, as was done with the Kansas scenes in MGM's The Wizard of Oz (1939). Television prints of the film were entirely in black-and-white. The sepia was intended to suggest the sweltering heat of the jungles in Panama.

The beautifully crafted costumes were made for an Errol Flynn film from the previous year, The Private Lives of Elizabeth and Essex (1939). Reusing them saved Warner Bros. a huge amount of money, since the costumes were heavily researched, meticulously created and very expensive.

Goofs

At the beginning of the movie during King Phillip's monologue, the map on the wall shows western and northern parts of the North American continent which were not known at the time.

When what's left of Captain Thorpe and his men are coming back to their ship after being ambushed by the Spanish, you can see the shadow of a boom mic on the upper right portion of the ship on the screen.

The story takes place in 1588. The flint-lock muskets and pistols used in the film were not in use until two-hundred years later.

The Letter. Leslie Crosbie, the wife of a Malayan rubber plantation owner, shoots and kills a neighbor she claims had dropped in to see her unexpectedly and made improper advances towards her. Her husband Robert was away for the night and no one has any treason to disbelieve her. They must go to Singapore however where the Attorney General decides she must stand trial for murder.

She has strong support from the British expatriate community but her solicitor Howard Joyce learns from his clerk that Leslie had in fact written to the dead man asking him to visit her that evening. The original of the letter is in the hands of the dead man's Eurasian widow and she wants a hefty amount to part with it. Although she survives the trial, Leslie must pay a far greater price in the end.

Nominated for 7 Oscars

Box Office
Cumulative Worldwide Gross: $16,455

Run time 1h 35mins

Trivia

After shooting was completed, William Wyler watched a rough cut and decided that he wanted the character of Leslie to be more sympathetic. He ordered some re-writes and planned to shoot them. Bette Davis recalled - "I was heartbroken," she said, "As I felt, after reading the rewrites, that my performance could be ruined with these additions. I asked Willie if I could see the film before doing the retakes. To my horror I was crying at myself at the end of the showing. There was dead silence in the projection room when the lights came up. I said, 'If we film these retakes, we will lose the intelligent audience. It is impossible to please everyone with any one film. If we try to accomplish this, we can lose all audiences.' Plus, to my shame, even though I played the part, I deeply sympathized with Leslie Crosbie. We only made one small addition to the original film. Wyler had agreed with me. Thank God!"

In filming the opening murder scene, actor David Newell had to roll down the stairs eight times after being shot, before director William Wyler was satisfied with the scene.

Just months after the film was released, James Stephenson died suddenly of a heart attack at the age of 53.

Goofs

The motor vehicles throughout are all left-hand drive. In Singapore traffic drives on the left and all vehicles there are right-hand drive.

We see Leslie faint and taken to see the nurse. The nurse leaves the room and Leslie is talking to Howard Joyce, but behind Mr. Joyce is a shadow of a piece of equipment or crew visible on the room divider behind Mr. Joyce. The equipment is pulled back and the shadow disappears.

MUSIC 1940

Artist and songs that have been number one throughout the year

Artist	Single	Reached number one	Weeks at number one
1940			
Frankie Masters	Scatter Brain	26th November 1939	8
Tommy Dorsey	All the thing Are Good	21st January 1940	2
Glenn Miller	In The Mood	4th February 1940	12
Glenn Miller	The Woodpecker Song	28th April 1940	7
Glenn Miller	Imagination	16th June 1940	3
Mitchell Ayers	Make Believe Island	7th July 1940	1
Glenn Miller	Fools Rush In	14th July 1940	1
Tommy Dorsey	I'll Never Smile Again	21st July 1940	12
Bing Crosby	Only Forever	13th October 1940	9
Artie Shaw	Frenesi	15th December 1940	13

Bing Crosby was the leading figure of the crooner sound as well as its most iconic, defining artist. By the 1940s, he was an entertainment superstar who mastered all of the major media formats of the day, movies, radio, and recorded music. Other popular singers of the day included Cab Calloway and Eddie Cantor.

Bandleaders such as the Dorsey Brothers often helped launch the careers of vocalists who went on to popularity as solo artists, such as Frank Sinatra, who rose to fame as a singer during this time. Sinatra's vast appeal to the "bobby soxers" revealed a whole new audience for popular music, which had generally appealed mainly to adults up to that time, making Sinatra the first teen idol. Sinatra's music mostly attracted young girls to his concerts. This image of a teen idol would also be seen with future artists such as Elvis Presley and The Beatles. Sinatra's massive popularity was also one of the reasons why the big band music declined in popularity; major record companies were looking for crooners and pop singers to attract a youth audience due to his success. Frank Sinatra would go on to become one of the most successful artists of the 1940s and one of the bestselling music artists of all time. Sinatra remained relevant through the 1950s and 60s, even with rock music being the dominant form of music in his later years. In the later decades, Sinatra's music would be mostly aimed at an older adult audience. Sinatra became one of the most respected and critically acclaimed music artists of all time.

Frankie Masters

"Scatter Brain"

"Scatter Brain" Frankie Masters was born on the April 12, 1904, USA. He began playing music while at college, eventually dropping out to become the leader of a theatre house band in Chicago, Illinois, USA. Several years later, in the late 20s, he decided to inaugurate his first dance band under his own name. Masters became a national celebrity when "Scatterbrain" became a major hit single, producing high profile engagements at the Pennsylvania Taft and Essex House hotels in New York. By the 40s they were among the most successful dance bands of their generation, with Masters acquiring a regular slot on Coca Cola Company's Victory Parade Of Spotlight Bands. After the end of World War II the band moved to the St. Francis Hotel in California, before returning to Chicago and the Stevens Hotel.

Tommy Dorsey

"All The Things Are Good"

"All the things are good". By 1939, Dorsey was aware of criticism that his band lacked a jazz feeling. He hired arranger Sy Oliver away from the Jimmie Lunceford band. Sy Oliver's arrangements include "On The Sunny Side of the Street" and "T.D.'s Boogie Woogie"; Oliver also composed two of the new band's signature instrumentals, "Well, Git It" and "Opus One". In 1940, Dorsey hired singer Frank Sinatra from bandleader Harry James. Frank Sinatra made eighty recordings from 1940 to 1942 with the Dorsey band. Two of those eighty songs are "In the Blue of Evening" and "This Love of Mine". Frank Sinatra achieved his first great success as a vocalist in the Dorsey band and claimed he learned breath control from watching Dorsey play trombone. In turn, Dorsey said his trombone style was heavily influenced by that of Jack Teagarden.

Glenn Miller

"In The Mood"

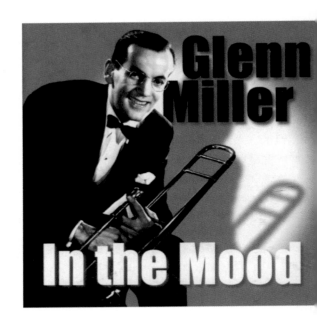

"I The Mood" "is a popular big band-era No. 1 hit recorded by American bandleader Glenn Miller. It topped the charts for 12 straight weeks in 1940 in the U.S. and one year later was featured in the movie Sun Valley Serenade. "In the Mood" is based on the composition "Tar Paper Stomp" by Wingy Manone. The first recording under the name "In the Mood" was released by Edgar Hayes & His Orchestra in 1938. "In the Mood" starts with a saxophone section theme based on repeated arpeggios that are rhythmically displaced; trumpets and trombones add accent riffs. The song was sold in 1939 to Glenn Miller, who experimented with the arrangement. The author of the final arrangement is unknown. One possibility is Eddie Durham because he wrote other arrangements on the same day that "In the Mood" was recorded.

Glenn Miller

"The Woodpecker Song"

"The Woodpecker Song". Is originally an Italian song. The music was written by Eldo Di Lazzaro in 1939, while the Italian lyrics were written by Bruno Cherubini. The English lyrics were written by Harold Adamson. The song became a hit in 1940, recorded by Glenn Miller and His Orchestra, The Andrews Sisters, and Kate Smith in 1940.

The Glenn Miller recording on RCA Bluebird featuring Marion Hutton on vocals reached #1 on the Billboard charts in 1940.

Glenn Miller

"Imagination"

"Imagination" is a popular song with music written by Jimmy Van Heusen and the lyrics by Johnny Burke. The song was first published in 1940. The two best-selling versions were recorded by the orchestras of Glenn Miller and Tommy Dorsey in 1940.

This was Glenn Millers third straight number one in the same year.

Mitchell Ayers

"Make Believe Island"

"Make Believe Island". In 1939, Bluebird Records offered the band an initial one-year contract; the arrangement lasted until 1942. All the while, the orchestra continued to function as a company, with the musician shareholders discussing business matters and voting on them. By 1940, the orchestra had its own show on CBS Radio. Ayres and the band appeared in three 1940s films: Swing time Johnny, Moonlight and Cactus, and Lady, Let's Dance.

Ayres and his orchestra reached the national number one spot for one week with their version of "Make Believe Island" (1940), vocal by Mary Ann Mercer.

Glenn Miller

"Fools Rush In"

"Fools Rush In" is a popular song. The lyrics were written by Johnny Mercer with music by Rube Bloom. The major hits at the time of introduction were Tony Martin, Glenn Miller with Ray Eberle, and Tommy Dorsey with Frank Sinatra. It was also recorded by Billy Eckstine. The song proved popular with 1960s pop and rhythm and blues artists, resulting in charted remakes in 1960 (Brook Benton), 1962 (Etta James), and 1963 (Ricky Nelson). The Ricky Nelson version was an enormous hit, reaching #12 on the Billboard pop chart and would become the most famous version of this song, and was featured in Kenneth Anger's film Scorpio Rising (1963). For their 1962 album Duet, Doris Day and André Previn recorded their interpretation of the song. Elvis Presley followed Ricky Nelson's style in 1971 as featured on the 1972 album Elvis Now.

Tommy Dorsey

"I'll Never Smile Again"

"I'll Never Smile Again" is a 1940 song written by Ruth Lowe. It has been recorded by many other artists since, becoming a standard.

The most successful and best-known version of the song was recorded by Tommy Dorsey and His Orchestra, with vocals provided by Frank Sinatra and The Pied Pipers. This recording was released as a Victor 78, 26628A, in 1940. This version was number one on Billboard's first "National List of Best Selling Retail Records" — the first official national music chart — on July 27, 1940, staying at the top spot for 12 weeks until October 12, 1940. The tune was inducted into the Grammy Hall of Fame in 1982.

Glenn Miller and His Orchestra also recorded a version of the song in 1940 on RCA Bluebird.

Bing Crosby

"Only Forever"

"Only Forever" is a song popularized in 1940 by Bing Crosby. It reached number one on the Billboard charts on October 19, 1940 and spent nine weeks in that position during a 20-week stay in the charts. "Only Forever" was written by James V. Monaco and Johnny Burke for the 1940 film Rhythm on the River and the song was nominated for the Academy Award for Best Original Song.

Crosby recorded it for Decca Records on July 3, 1940 with John Scott Trotter and His Orchestra. Tommy Dorsey and Eddy Duchin also enjoyed chart success with the song. The song has also been recorded by Anne Shelton, Dean Martin, Kay Starr, Nat King Cole, Vera Lynn and Al Bowlly & Jimmy Mesene.

Artie Shaw

"Frenesi"

"Frenesí" is a musical piece originally composed by Alberto Domínguez for the marimba, and adapted as a jazz standard by Leonard Whitcup and others. The word frenesí is Spanish for "frenzy".

A hit version recorded by Artie Shaw and His Orchestra (with an arrangement by William Grant Still) reached number one on the Billboard pop chart on the December 21, 1940, staying for thirteen weeks and was inducted into the Grammy Hall of Fame in 1982.

The Shaw recording was used in the soundtrack of the 1980 film Raging Bull.

WORLD EVENTS

January

1st The Winter War, the Battle of Raate Road began. The Winter War was a military conflict between the Soviet Union (USSR) and Finland. It began with a Soviet invasion of Finland on the 30th November 1939, three months after the outbreak of World War II, and ended three and a half months later with the Moscow Peace Treaty on the 13th March 1940. The League of Nations deemed the attack illegal and expelled the Soviet Union from the organization.

2nd The Irish government introduced emergency powers to incarcerate members of the Irish Republican Army without trial.

3rd U.S. President Franklin D. Roosevelt gave the 1940 State of the Union Address to Congress. "In previous messages to the Congress I have repeatedly warned that, whether we like it or not, the daily lives of American citizens will, of necessity, feel the shock of events on other continents. This is no longer mere theory; because it has been definitely proved to us by the facts of yesterday and today," the president said. He asked the Congress to approve increased national defense spending "based not on panic but on common sense" and "to levy sufficient additional taxes" to help pay for it.

7th German documents record an attack on this date by the German First Minesweeper Flotilla on an unidentified submarine near Heligoland. Since the British submarine Seahorse was on patrol at the time but never returned, it is thought to have been sunk in this attack.

9th During the war, Starfish, part of the 2nd Submarine Flotilla, conducted five uneventful war patrols in the North Sea. On the 9th January 1940, during her sixth patrol, she attacked a German minesweeper off Heligoland Bight, but after the attack failed and her diving planes jammed, Starfish was repeatedly attacked with depth charges. Badly damaged, she was forced to surface, and sank after all her crew was rescued by German ships.

January

11th   The Sergei Prokofiev ballet Romeo and Juliet made its Russian debut at the Korov Theatre in Leningrad amid wartime blackout conditions.

12th   The Danish tanker Danmark was torpedoed and sunk by the German submarine U-23 off the Orkney Islands. The crew of 40 escaped safely.

13th   The Finnish escort Aura II was sunk by its own depth charge trying to attack a Soviet submarine in the Sea of Åland.

14th   Hitler ordered that no one would be allowed to know more than he did about any secret matter.

17th   Europe was struck by a cold wave. In Finland the mercury dipped as low as –45 degrees Celsius, while in England the River Thames froze up for the first time since 1888.

19th   The British destroyer Grenville struck a mine in the Thames Estuary and sank. 77 lives were lost but 108 were rescued.

20th   Winston Churchill gave an address over the radio referred to as the "House of Many Mansions" speech, with neutral nations its primary subject. Churchill explained that there was "no chance of a speedy end" to the war "except through united action," and asked listeners to consider what would happen if neutral nations "were with one spontaneous impulse to do their duty in accordance with the Covenant of the League, and were to stand together with the British and French Empires against aggression and wrong?" Churchill concluded, "The day will come when the joy bells will ring again throughout Europe, and when victorious nations, masters not only of their foes but of themselves, will plan and build in justice, in tradition, and in freedom a house of many mansions where there will be room for all."

21st   The British destroyer Exmouth was sunk in the Moray Firth with the loss of all hands by the German submarine U-22.

23rd   Britain lowered the speed limit at night in populated areas to 20 miles per hour due to the sharp increase in the rate of auto accidents during blackouts.

24th   The German government ordered the registration of all Jewish-owned property in Poland.

January

25th France announced a new decree providing sentences of up to two years in prison and fines up to 5,000 francs for "false assertions" presented as "personal opinions" that correspond to "enemy propaganda and which, expressed publicly, indicate the marked intention of their authors to injure national defense by attacking the morale of the army and population."

26th U-boat captains were permitted from now on to make submerged attacks without warning on certain merchant vessels (though not on Spanish, Russian, Japanese or American ships) east of Scotland, in the Bristol Channel and in the English Channel.

27th The German government demanded at least 1 million industrial and rural workers be provided from Nazi occupied Poland to work assignments in the Reich.

28th A new musical quiz show called Beat the Band premiered on NBC Radio. The audience sent in riddles to the house band in which the answer was always the title of a song. Listeners earned $10 if their question was used and an additional $10 if their question stumped the band.

29th Actress Jill Esmond won a divorce from her husband Laurence Olivier. Vivien Leigh was named as co-respondent and Olivier did not contest the proceedings.

30th Adolf Hitler gave a speech at the Berlin Sportpalast on the seventh anniversary of the Nazis taking power, his first formal address since narrowly avoiding the attempt on his life in November. The location of the speech was kept secret up until a few hours before it began. Hitler claimed that Britain and France "wanted war" and he vowed that they would "get their fight."

31st Britain secretly approached neutral Italy about purchasing badly needed fighter planes for the war effort. Germany would ensure that no such deal would be made.

February

1st Japan passed a massive budget devoting unprecedented sums to weapons and training.

3rd A German plane crashed on English soil for the first time in the war when a Heinkel He 111 was shot down near Whitby. Flight Lieutenant Peter Townsend of 43 Squadron was credited with the air victory.

5th The Anglo-French Supreme War Council met again in Paris with Neville Chamberlain and Winston Churchill in attendance. Franco-British plans for intervention in the Winter War were discussed.

6th The "Careless Talk Costs Lives" propaganda campaign began in Britain, aimed at preventing war gossip.

7th The Walt Disney animated film Pinocchio premiered at the Center Theatre in New York City.

8th Neville Chamberlain made a speech in Parliament updating the House on the general international situation, saying there was "no reason to be dissatisfied" with the early progress of the war. Chamberlain also praised the Finnish people for their "heroic struggle" that "has evoked the admiration of the world" and said that "further aid is now on its way."

February

9th | Joe Louis defeated Arturo Godoy by split decision at Madison Square Garden in New York City to retain the world heavyweight boxing title.

10th | From the south portico of the White House, U.S. President Franklin D. Roosevelt confronted a gathering of 4,500 members of the American Youth Congress, which had recently passed a resolution declaring that granting aid to Finland was an "attempt to force America into the imperialistic war" against the Soviet Union. Roosevelt told them that it was "a grand thing" for youth to be interested enough in government to come to Washington, but offered "some words of warning or perhaps I should say of suggestion ... do not as a group pass resolutions on subjects which you have not thought through and on which you cannot possibly have complete knowledge." The president continued, "That American sympathy is ninety-eight per cent with the Finns in their effort to stave off invasion of their own soil is by now axiomatic. That America wants to help them by lending or giving money to them to save their own lives is also axiomatic today. That the Soviet Union would, because of this, declare war on the United States is about the silliest thought that I have ever heard advanced in the fifty-eight years of my life. That we are going to war ourselves with the Soviet Union is an equally silly thought." The organization responded by booing the president, but the event was politically useful to Roosevelt in that it served as a rejoinder to accusations from his opponents that he was sympathetic to communism.

12th | German submarine U-33 was sunk in the Firth of Clyde by the minesweeper Gleaner. 25 of the crew perished but there were 17 survivors, one of which had three Enigma machine rotors in his pockets which were sent to Alan Turing at the Government Code and Cypher School for study.

13th | Finland asked Sweden to provide troops to fight against the Soviet Union, but Sweden refused out of fear that both Britain and Germany would respond by invading Sweden.

16th | In Egypt, the British Army created the 7th Armored Division, later to be famous as the "Desert Rats".

17th | Germany accused Britain of "piracy, murder and gangsterism" over the Altmark incident and also lodged a protest with Norway demanding compensation for failing to protect the German ship within Norwegian territorial waters. Norway in turn protested to Britain for infringing on the country's neutrality.

21st | The results of a Gallup poll were published asking Americans, "If it appears that Germany is defeating England and France, should the United States declare war on Germany and send our army and navy to Europe to fight?" 77% said no and 23% said yes, not counting the 7% who expressed no opinion.

22nd | The Kriegsmarine launched Operation Wikinger, targeting British fishing vessels suspected of reporting the movements of German warships. En route, the destroyer flotilla was mistakenly bombed by a Heinkel He 111, sinking the Leberecht Maass and killing 280 aboard. The Max Schultz hit a naval mine attempting a rescue effort and also sank with the loss of all 308 crew.

24th | Speaking in his home city of Birmingham in an address broadcast to the United States, Neville Chamberlain outlined Britain's aims: the independence of the Poles and Czechs, and "tangible evidence to satisfy us that pledges and assurances when they are given will be fulfilled ... Therefore, it is for Germany to take the next step and to show us conclusively that she has abandoned that thesis that might is right."

February

25th | The first squadron of the Royal Canadian Air Force arrived in Britain.

26th | The large passenger liner RMS Queen Elizabeth left Clydebank on a secret maiden voyage to New York for her final fitting. The British generated false intelligence to make the Germans believe that the ship's destination was Southampton.

27th | Norway and Sweden refused to allow British and French troops to cross through their territory to aid Finland.

29th | The 12th Academy Awards were held in Los Angeles, hosted by Bob Hope for the first of what would be nineteen times. Gone With the Wind won eight awards including Best Picture. Hattie McDaniel became the first African-American to win an Oscar when she was named Best Supporting Actress. The Los Angeles Times published the names of the winners in its 8:45 p.m. edition, so most of the attendees already knew the results ahead of time. The Academy would respond by starting a tradition the following year in which the winners were not revealed until the ceremony itself when sealed envelopes were opened.

March

1st | In Germany, the second stop of U.S. Undersecretary of State Sumner Welles' fact-finding mission, he met with Joachim von Ribbentrop and listened to him speak almost non-stop for two hours. Welles came away thinking that Ribbentrop had a "completely closed mind" that was "also a very stupid mind."

2nd | Sumner Welles went to the Chancellery and met Adolf Hitler, who claimed to want peace but insisted that Britain was determined to destroy Germany. Welles' impression of Hitler was that he appeared to be calm and in excellent health and that "while his eyes were tired, they were clear."

3rd | Sumner Welles met Hermann Göring at Carinhall. Like Hitler, Göring blamed the war on Britain and France. Welles found Göring to be as cold and ruthless as the other Nazi leaders but thought he was at least capable of taking a broader view of international relations.

4th | The Home Office announced that women would not be asked to work more than 60 hours a week in British factories, and youth under 16 would not be required to work more than 48. In World War I, women were frequently working as many as 70 hours a week.

5th | In the English Channel, the Royal Navy seized seven Italian ships leaving Germany loaded with coal.

7th | The RMS Queen Elizabeth completed her secret maiden voyage from England to New York.

9th | Britain released the captured Italian coal ships and announced that Italy would be allowed to continue to import German coal, but only via overland routes.

11th | The French battleship Bretagne and cruiser Algérie departed Toulon with 147 tons worth of gold, bound for Canada where the French gold reserves would be kept for safekeeping.

March

12th | Sumner Welles met Winston Churchill. In Welles' account of the meeting he wrote that "Mr. Churchill was sitting in front of the fire, smoking a 24-inch cigar, and drinking a whiskey and soda. It was quite obvious that he had consumed a good many whiskeys before I arrived." For almost two hours Welles listened to Churchill deliver "a cascade of oratory, brilliant and always effective, interlarded with considerable wit."

16th | A British civilian was killed in a German air raid for the first time in the war when fourteen Junkers Ju 88 bombers attacked the British fleet at Scapa Flow.

18th | Hitler met with Mussolini at the Brenner Pass in the Alps. Hitler made it clear that German troops were poised to launch an offensive in the west and that Mussolini would have to decide whether Italy would join in the attack or not. Since Italy was still not ready for war, Mussolini suggested that the offensive could be delayed a few more months, to which Hitler replied that Germany was not altering its plans to suit Italy. The two agreed that Italy would come into the war in due course.

21st | The ocean liner Queen Mary departed New York City for Sydney to be refitted as a troopship.

RMS Queen Mary

23rd | Twelve Irish Republican Army convicts rioted in HM Prison Dartmoor. The inmates took two warders prisoner, locked a third one in a cell and started a fire that took 90 minutes to put out.

24th | The French destroyer La Railleuse was sunk off Casablanca by the accidental explosion of one of its own torpedoes. 28 crewmen were killed and 24 wounded.

March

25th | The British government ordered its troops not to participate in German radio broadcasts if they became prisoners of war. Britons had been tuning in to German radio to learn of the capture of family members by hearing their voices, long before information of their capture could reach the British government.

28th | The Anglo-French Supreme War Council met in London and agreed that neither Britain nor France would make a separate peace with Germany. The Council also agreed upon Operation Wilfred, a plan to lay mines in Norwegian coastal waters in the hopes of provoking a German response that would legitimize Allied "assistance" to Norway.

31st | Winston Churchill gave a speech over the radio titled "Dwelling in the Cage with the Tiger", a metaphor he used to describe the precarious geographical situation of the Dutch. As with his January 20 speech, Churchill primarily spoke about neutral countries and said, "It might have been a very short war, perhaps; indeed, there might have been no war, if all the neutral States, who share our conviction upon fundamental matters, and who openly or secretly, sympathize with us, had stood together at one signal and in one line. We did not count on this, we did not expect it, and therefore we are not disappointed or dismayed ... But the fact is that many of the smaller States of Europe are terrorized by Nazi violence and brutality into supplying Germany with the material of modern war, and this fact may condemn the whole world to a prolonged ordeal with grievous, unmeasured consequences in many lands." In the wake of the Altmark Incident and with Operation Wilfred about to go into action, Churchill said of Germany's neutral neighbors that "we understand their dangers and their point of view, but it would not be right, or in the general interest, that their weakness should be the aggressor's strength, and fill to overflowing the cup of human woe. There could be no justice if in a moral struggle the aggressor tramples down every sentiment of humanity, and if those who resist him remain entangled in the tatters of violated legal conventions."

April

1st | The BBC broadcast what appeared to be a speech by Adolf Hitler, in which the Führer reminded the audience that Columbus had discovered America with the help of German science and technology, and therefore Germany had a right "to have some part in the achievement which this voyage of discovery was to result in." This meant that all Americans of Czech and Polish descent were entitled to come under the protection of Germany and that Hitler would "enforce that right, not only theoretically but practically." Once the German Protectorate was extended to the United States, the Statue of Liberty would be removed to alleviate traffic congestion and the White House would be renamed the Brown House. CBS contacted the BBC in something of a panic trying to learn more about the origin of the broadcast, not realizing that it was an April Fools' Day hoax. The voice of Hitler had been impersonated by the actor Martin Miller.

2nd | Adolf Hitler signed the order for Operation Weserübung, the German invasion of Denmark and Norway.

3rd | The British cabinet approved Operation Wilfred, Winston Churchill's plan to mine the sea routes between Norway, Sweden and Germany and for Anglo-French landings in Norway to forestall a German invasion there, which British intelligence believed, was imminent. However, the British government still dithered about implementing the plan due to Norway's neutrality.

April

4th   Neville Chamberlain gave a speech to the Conservative Party in London stating he was confident of victory and that Hitler had "missed the bus" by not taking advantage of Germany's military superiority over Britain at the beginning of the war.

7th   British reconnaissance aircraft spotted a large German naval force heading northward. RAF bombers were dispatched to attack the group but this attack was not successful.

8th   The British destroyer Glowworm was sunk by the German cruiser Admiral Hipper in the Norwegian Sea. Despite being hopelessly outgunned, the Glowworm managed to ram the Admiral Hipper and inflict considerable damage before sinking. Captain Gerard Broadmead Roope (below) earned the first Victoria Cross of the war for his conduct, but it was only bestowed after the war when the Admiral Hipper's log describing the battle was read by the Royal Navy.

9th   The French and British put Plan R 4 into action. Plan R 4 was the World War II British plan for an invasion of the neutral states of Norway and Sweden in April 1940, in the event of Germany violating the territorial integrity of Norway. Earlier, the British had planned a similar intervention with France during the Winter War.

11th   First Lord of the Admiralty Winston Churchill made a speech to the House of Commons announcing that the strategically important Faroe Islands belonging to Denmark were now being occupied by Britain. "We shall shield the Faroe Islands from all the severities of war and establish ourselves there conveniently by sea and air until the moment comes when they will be handed back to the Crown and people of a Denmark liberated from the foul thralldom in which they have been plunged by the German aggression," Churchill said.

12th   The Alfred Hitchcock-directed psychological-thriller mystery film Rebecca premiered in the United States.

13th   Eight German destroyers and the submarine U-64 were sunk or scuttled during the Second Battle of Narvik.

15th | The British 146th Infantry Brigade landed at Namsos and started to advance south towards Trondheim. Further north, other British troops landed in the Lofoten Islands.

17th | The British cruiser Suffolk shelled a German held-airfield at Stavanger, but was attacked by aircraft in return, heavily damaged and put out of action for almost a year.

19th | At Verdal, British and German land forces engaged each other for the first time in the war.

20th | The British 148th Infantry Brigade arrived at Lillehammer and began moving south. The British supply base at Namsos came under bombing from German forces, but there was little the British could do to fight back as they were short on anti-aircraft weaponry.

23rd | On Budget Day in the United Kingdom, Chancellor of the Exchequer Sir John Simon announced that the government was seeking an all-time record £1.234 billion in revenue to meet the cost of the war through March 1941. Taxes and duties were increased on income, alcohol, tobacco, telephone calls, telegrams of "ordinary priority" and postage.

24th | Issue #1 of the comic book Batman was published, starring the character of the same name that was already popular from his appearances in other comics over the previous year. This first issue marked the debut of the Joker and Cat woman (initially called The Cat).

April

25th   Women gained the right to vote in the Canadian province of Quebec, the last province to grant women's suffrage.

26th   The British 15th Brigade fell back 3 kilometers to Kjorem after their supplies were destroyed by a full day of bombing from the Germans, who had complete air superiority. London began seriously considering a complete withdrawal from Norway.

27th   Germany finally declared war on Norway. Joachim von Ribbentrop took to the airwaves shortly afterward and claimed that the Germans had captured documents from the Lillehammer sector revealing a British and French plan to occupy Norway with Norwegian complicity. That same day Samuel Hoare made a radio address of his own in which he called Ribbentrop's assertion "despicable."

28th   The British government ordered troops at Trondheim to withdraw as the 15th Brigade fell back again to Dombås.

29th   The 1940 Summer Olympics, officially known as the Games of the XII Olympiad, were originally scheduled to be held from 21st September to 6th October 1940, in Tokyo, Japan. They were rescheduled for Helsinki, Finland, to be held from the 20th July to 4th August 1940, but were ultimately cancelled due to the outbreak of World War II. Helsinki eventually hosted the 1952 Summer Olympics and Tokyo the 1964 Summer Olympics.

30th   The British sloop Bittern was severely damaged off Namsos by German dive-bombers. Allied ships rescued the survivors and then scuttled the ship with a torpedo from the destroyer Janus.

May

1st   Adolf Hitler set a date of May 6 for the western offensive. This date would be postponed a few more times prior to May 10 due to weather.

3rd   The Allied evacuation at Namsos was completed, but German aircraft located part of the evacuation fleet and sank the destroyers Afridi and Bison.

4th   The Polish destroyer Grom was sunk in the fjord Rombaken by a German Heinkel He 111.

 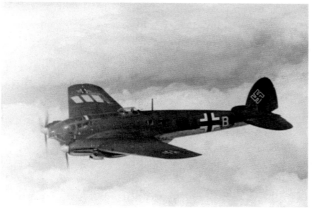

May

5th | RC Paris defeated Olympique de Marseille 2-1 in the Coupe de France Final.

6th | Unemployment in the United Kingdom fell below 1 million people for the first time in 20 years.

7th | Norway Debate: The British House of Commons began a contentious debate on the conduct of the war. Sir Roger Keyes dramatically appeared dressed in full military uniform with six rows of medals and described in detail the government's mishandling of the Norwegian campaign. Leo Amery stood and uttered the famous words, "Somehow or other we must get into the Government men who can match our enemies in fighting spirit, in daring, in resolution and in thirst for victory." After quoting Oliver Cromwell, he continued: "I will quote certain other words. I do it with great reluctance, because I am speaking of those who are old friends and associates of mine, but they are words which, I think, are applicable to the present situation. This is what Cromwell said to the Long Parliament when he thought it was no longer fit to conduct the affairs of the nation: 'You have sat too long here for any good you have been doing. Depart, I say, and let us have done with you. In the name of God, go!'"

8th | The Norway Debate continued in Parliament. David Lloyd George said that since Chamberlain had asked the nation for sacrifice, "I say solemnly that the Prime Minister should give an example of sacrifice, because there is nothing which can contribute more to victory in this war than that he should sacrifice the seals of office." Chamberlain survived a motion of no confidence by a vote of 281 to 200, but the number of abstentions from within his own Conservative Party caused the level of support for his government to appear very weak.

9th | The age of conscription in the United Kingdom was raised to 36.

Germany invaded France and the Low Countries at dawn. The Battles of France, the Netherlands, and Belgium began. U.S. President Franklin D. Roosevelt learned of the German attack at 11:00 p.m. on the 9th May, Washington time. He phoned his Treasury Secretary, Henry Morgenthau, Jr., and told him to freeze Belgian, Dutch, and Luxembourger assets in the United States to keep them out of Germany's hands. Roosevelt could do little more that night, since phone calls to Paris and Brussels were rarely getting through, so he went to bed at 2:40 a.m. Neville Chamberlain went to Buckingham Palace around 6:00 in the evening (18:00) and resigned as Prime Minister of the United Kingdom. King George VI asked Winston Churchill to form the next government, and Churchill accepted.

12th | Child star Shirley Temple, through her mother Gertrude Temple, cancelled her movie contract with 20th Century Fox and retired from film acting at age 11.

13th | Winston Churchill made his first speech to the House of Commons as Prime Minister. He famously said, "I have nothing to offer but blood, toil, tears, and sweat."

14th | French artillery and antitank guns hit Erwin Rommel's tank near the Belgian village of Onhaye. Rommel was wounded in the right cheek by a small shell splinter as the tank slid down a slope and rolled over on its side, but he escaped serious injury.

15th | Churchill sent a message to Roosevelt asking for a one-year loan of forty or fifty older destroyers as well as aircraft, antiaircraft guns and steel. President Roosevelt sent a message back to Churchill explaining that a loan of destroyers would require an act of Congress, but generally agreeing on the other matters.

May

17th	The German 6th Army captured Brussels.
18th	Rommel's 7th Panzer Division captured Cambrai through deception. Rommel ordered his tanks and self-propelled guns to drive across the open fields and create as much dust as possible, creating the illusion that the advancing force was much larger than it actually was. The defenders abandoned the town without firing a shot.
19th	Winston Churchill made his first broadcast to the British people as Prime Minister. Churchill acknowledged that the Germans were making swift progress and that it would be "foolish ... to disguise the gravity of the hour," but said that only a "very small part" of the French Army had yet been heavily engaged. Churchill explained that he had formed an "Administration of men and women of every Party and of almost every point of view. We have differed and quarreled in the past; but now one bond unites us all - to wage war until victory is won, and never to surrender ourselves to servitude and shame, whatever the cost and the agony may be." The speech was titled Be ye men of valor, after a quotation from 1 Maccabees in the Apocrypha.
21st	The Battle of Arras took place on the 21st May 1940, during the Battle of France in the Second World War. British and French tanks and infantry advanced south from Arras to force back German armored forces, which were advancing westwards down the Somme river valley towards the English Channel, to trap the Allied forces in northern France and Belgium. The Anglo-French attack made early gains and panicked some German units but was repulsed after an advance of up to 6.2 mi (10 km) and forced to withdraw after dark to avoid encirclement.
22nd	Britain passed the Emergency Powers (Defense) Act 1940 putting banks, munitions production, wages, profits and work conditions under the control of the state.
24th	On Empire Day, King George VI addressed his subjects by radio, saying, "The decisive struggle is now upon us ... Let no one be mistaken; it is not mere territorial conquest that our enemies are seeking. It is the overthrow, complete and final, of this Empire and of everything for which it stands, and after that the conquest of the world. And if their will prevails they will bring to its accomplishment all the hatred and cruelty which they have already displayed."
25th	The British aircraft carrier Illustrious was commissioned.
26th	Benito Mussolini met with Army Chief of Staff Pietro Badoglio and Air Marshal Italo Balbo in Rome. Mussolini told them that Italy would have to enter the war soon if it wanted a place at the peace conference table when the spoils were divided up. Badoglio tactfully tried to explain that Italy was still unprepared for war, pointing out that there were not even enough shirts for all the soldiers. Mussolini snapped back, "History cannot be reckoned by the number of shirts." He set June 5th as the date for the Italian invasion of France.
27th	The Dunkirk evacuation codenamed Operation Dynamo began. The first 7,669 British troops were evacuated.
28th	Belgium surrendered unconditionally to Germany at 4 a.m. A bad-tempered Paul Reynaud announced in a radio address that day that "France can no longer count on the Belgian Army" and said the surrender had been made without consulting the British or French governments.

May

29th | The Germans captured Lille, Ostend and Ypres and 33,558 were evacuated from Dunkirk.

30th | In the wake of the previous day's losses, the British Admiralty ordered all modern destroyers to depart Dunkirk and leave 18 older destroyers to continue the evacuation. A total of 53,823 were evacuated on this day.

31st | Poor weather over Dunkirk allowed the British to conduct the day's evacuations with reduced fear of German air attacks. This day was the high point of the evacuation, with a total of 68,014 rescued.

June

1st | German bombers sank the French destroyer Foudroyant off Dunkirk as the evacuation from there continued. A total of 64,429 were evacuated on this day.

2nd | War Secretary Anthony Eden gave a radio address on the Dunkirk evacuation reporting that four-fifths of the British Expeditionary Force had been saved. "The British Expeditionary Force still exists, not as a handful of fugitives, but as a body of seasoned veterans," Eden said. "We have had great losses in equipment. But our men have gained immeasurably in experience of warfare and in self-confidence. The vital weapon of any army is its spirit. Ours has been tried and tempered in the furnace. It has not been found wanting. It is this refusal to accept defeat that is the guarantee of final victory." 26,256 were evacuated from Dunkirk as operations switched to only being undertaken at night due to the costly air attacks.

3rd | The last British troops were evacuated from Dunkirk.

4th | The Battle of Dunkirk ended with the overnight evacuation of 26,175 French troops. At 10:20 a.m. the Germans occupied the city and captured the 30–40,000 French troops who were left.

5th | The Germans began the second phase of the invasion of France, codenamed Fall Rot, by attacking across the Somme and Aisne rivers. The Germans initially met stiff resistance, since the French had spent the past two weeks organizing their defenses south of the Somme.

7th | A single airplane from the French Navy bombed Berlin in a night raid. The Farman 223.4 lingered over the city for as long as possible to create the impression of more than one airplane, and then dropped its bomb load over some factories in Berlin's north end.

8th | The German 5th and 7th Panzer Divisions crossed the Seine River. The 5th Panzer Division captured Rouen.

9th | The French government fled Paris.

10th | At 6 p.m., Benito Mussolini appeared on the balcony of the Palazzo Venezia to announce that in six hours, Italy would be in a state of war with France and Britain. After a speech explaining his motives for the decision, he concluded: "People of Italy: take up your weapons and show your tenacity, your courage and your valor." The Italians had no battle plans of any kind prepared. Anti-Italian riots broke out in major cities across the United Kingdom after Italy's declaration of war. Bricks, stones and bottles were thrown through the windows of Italian-owned shops, and 100 arrests were made in Edinburgh alone.

11th   Rommel's 7th Panzer Division reached Le Havre, then turned back to trap 46,000 British and French soldiers at Saint-Valery-en-Caux.

12th   After a last stand, the outflanked 51st Highland Division and French 9th Army Corps surrendered to Rommel at Saint-Valery-en-Caux.

14th   The first inmates of Auschwitz and Theresienstadt concentration camp arrived.

15th   Operation Aerial was the evacuation of Allied forces and civilians from ports in western France from 15th to 25th June 1940 during the Second World War. The evacuation followed the military collapse in the Battle of France against Nazi Germany, after Operation Dynamo, the evacuation from Dunkirk and Operation Cycle, an embarkation from Le Havre, which finished on the 13th June. British and Allied ships were covered from French bases by five Royal Air Force fighter squadrons and assisted by aircraft based in England, to lift British, Polish and Czech troops, civilians and equipment from Atlantic ports, particularly from St Nazaire and Nantes.

The Luftwaffe attacked the evacuation ships and on the 17th June, evaded RAF fighter patrols and sank the Cunard liner and troopship HMT Lancastria in the Loire estuary. The ship sank quickly and vessels in the area were still under attack during rescue operations, which saved about 2,477 passengers and crew. The liner had thousands of troops, RAF personnel and civilians on board and the number of the passengers who died in the sinking is unknown, because in the haste to embark as many people as possible, keeping count broke down. The loss of at least 3,500 people made the disaster the greatest loss of life in a British ship, which the British government tried to keep secret on the orders of Winston Churchill, the British Prime Minister.

18th   "This was their finest hour" was a speech delivered by Winston Churchill to the House of Commons of the United Kingdom on the 18th June 1940, just over a month after he took over as Prime Minister at the head of an all-party coalition government.

It was the third of three speeches which he gave during the period of the Battle of France, after the "Blood, toil, tears and sweat" speech of the 13th May and the "We shall fight on the beaches" speech of the 4th June. "This was their finest hour" was made after France had sought an armistice on the evening of the 16th June.

June

19th | Charles de Gaulle broadcast again over the BBC. "Faced by the bewilderment of my countrymen, by the disintegration of a government in thrall to the enemy, by the fact that the institutions of my country are incapable, at the moment, of functioning, I, General de Gaulle, a French soldier and military leader, realize that I now speak for France," he said. "In the name of France, I make the following solemn declaration: It is the bounden duty of all Frenchmen who still bear arms to continue the struggle. For them to lay down their arms, to evacuate any position of military importance, or agree to hand over any part of French territory, however small, to enemy control, would be a crime against our country. For the moment I refer particularly to French North Africa - to the integrity of French North Africa."

20th | The first Australian and New Zealand troops arrived in the United Kingdom.

21st | At about 3:15 p.m., peace negotiations between France and Germany began at the Glade of the Armistice in the Forest of Compiègne, using the same rail carriage that the Armistice of the 11th November 1918 was signed in. Adolf Hitler personally attended the negotiations at first, but left early as a show of disrespect to the French. A point of contention was the size of the zone that the Germans were to occupy, so the war dragged on for another day.

23rd | Adolf Hitler took a train to Paris and visited sites including the Eiffel Tower, the Arc de Triomphe and Napoleon's tomb at Les Invalides.

25th | German troops were issued English phrase books in preparation for an invasion of Britain.

28th | The Germans bombed the harbors of Saint Helier and La Roque on the island of Jersey and Saint Peter Port Harbor on Guernsey, killing a total of 42 people.

30th | The Germans occupied the Channel Islands unopposed.

July

1st | The British government advised women to conserve wood by wearing shoes with flatter heels.

3rd | Cardiff Blitz: the first German air raid on Cardiff, Wales took place.

4th | Winston Churchill expressed "sincere sorrow" as he delivered a speech to the House of Commons explaining "the measures which we have felt bound to take in order to prevent the French Fleet from falling into German hands."

6th | The first U-boat base in France became operational at Lorient.

9th | The British House of Commons unanimously passed a £1 billion war credit.

10th | The Battle of Britain began. In its opening phase the Luftwaffe attacked coastal targets and shipping convoys in the English Channel with the goal of reducing Britain's air defenses and naval supply lines ahead of a general air offensive.

14th | Bastille Day in the unoccupied portion of France was observed solemnly with flags at half-mast.

July

19th Hitler made a speech to the Reichstag reviewing the course of the war and then warned, "Mr. Churchill, or perhaps others, for once believe me when I predict a great empire will be destroyed, an empire that it was never my intention to destroy or even to harm. I do realize that this struggle, if it continues, can end only with the complete annihilation of one or the other of the two adversaries. Mr. Churchill may believe this will be Germany. I know that it will be Britain." Hitler then appealed "once more to reason and common sense", saying, "I can see no reason why this war must go on." He said if Churchill brushed aside this appeal, "I shall have relieved my conscience in regard to the things to come."

20th The British government banned the buying and selling of new cars.

23rd Chancellor of the Exchequer Sir Kingsley Wood introduced Britain's third war budget. A 24 percent tax was imposed on luxuries.

24th The French passenger liner Meknés departed Southampton for Marseilles for repatriation of the 1,277 captured French Navy sailors aboard. The ship was torpedoed in the English Channel by the German torpedo boat S-27 despite the Meknés' displays of neutrality. Four British destroyers rescued the survivors but 416 perished.

25th A British coal convoy took heavy losses from German dive bombers. The Admiralty ordered future convoys to take place at night as a result.

27th Bugs Bunny made his debut in the animated short, A Wild Hare.

28th German fighter ace Werner Mölders was wounded in the legs by enemy fire during the Battle of Britain but managed to return to base at Wissant. Mölders spent the next month recovering in hospital.

29th German naval command issued a memo noting that the mid-September 1940 date for an invasion of Britain as demanded by Hitler was possible, but recommended a postponement to May 1941.

31st A conference was held at the Berghof between Hitler, Keitel, Jodl, Raeder, Brauchitsch, Halder and Puttkamer. Raeder reported that the navy would not be ready for Operation Sea Lion until mid-September, if then, so discussion turned to attacking the Soviet Union instead. Hitler believed that defeating Russia would make Germany unbeatable and force Britain to come to terms, so an invasion of the Soviet Union was set for spring 1941.

August

1st Hitler issued Directive No. 17, declaring his intention to intensify air and sea warfare against the English in order to "establish the necessary conditions for the final conquest of England."

4th American General John J. Pershing gave a nationwide radio broadcast urging that aid be sent to Britain. "It is not hysterical to insist that democracy and liberty are threatened," Pershing said. "Democracy and liberty have been overthrown on the continent of Europe. Only the British are left to defend democracy and liberty in Europe. By sending help to the British we can still hope with confidence to keep the war on the other side of the Atlantic Ocean, where the enemies of liberty, if possible, should be defeated."

August

7th Winston Churchill and Charles de Gaulle signed an agreement on the military organization of the Free French. Churchill agreed to allow the French units to have as much autonomy as possible.

9th The first air raid of the Birmingham Blitz took place when a single aircraft bombed Erdington.

12th The second phase of the Battle of Britain began as the Luftwaffe expanded its targets to include British airfields. Bf 110s and Stuka dive bombers attacked radar installations along the coastlines of Kent, Sussex and the Isle of Wight, damaging five radar stations and putting one out of action for eleven days.

13th The German military operation known as Adlertag was put into action with the goal of destroying the Royal Air Force, but the attempt failed.

15th In the biggest air engagement of the Battle of Britain up to this point, the Luftwaffe attempted to overwhelm the RAF with a series of major air attacks. The Germans lost 76 aircraft to the British 34, and to the Germans the day became known as Black Thursday.

16th The Spanish Surrealist artist Salvador Dalí and wife Gala arrived in New York to escape the war in Europe. They would not return to Europe for eight years.

17th Adolf Hitler ordered a total blockade of Britain as a means of weakening the island prior to Operation Sea Lion.

18th In the Battle of Britain the air battle known as The Hardest Day was fought, with an inconclusive result. The Germans lost 69 aircraft and the British 29. The Hardest Day is a name given to a Second World War air battle fought on the 18th August 1940 during the Battle of Britain between the German Luftwaffe and British Royal Air Force. On this day, the Luftwaffe made an all-out effort to destroy RAF Fighter Command. The air battles that took place on this day were amongst the largest aerial engagements in history to that time. Both sides suffered heavy losses. In the air, the British shot down twice as many Luftwaffe aircraft as they lost. However, many RAF aircraft were destroyed on the ground, equalizing the total losses of both sides. Further large and costly aerial battles took place after the 18th August, but both sides lost more aircraft combined on this day than at any other point during the campaign, including the 15th September, the Battle of Britain Day, generally considered the climax of the fighting. For this reason, the 18th August 1940 became known as "the Hardest Day" in Britain.

August

19th	The weather in Britain from this day through to August 23rd was wet with plenty of low cloud, causing a drop in the frequency of air raids. British ground crews took advantage of the lull in the fighting to repair damaged planes and airfields while Hermann Göring fumed at the loss of time.
20th	"Never was so much owed by so many to so few" was a wartime speech made by the British prime minister Winston Churchill on the 20th August 1940. The name stems from the specific line in the speech, Never in the field of human conflict was so much owed by so many to so few, referring to the ongoing efforts of the Royal Air Force crews who were at the time fighting the Battle of Britain, the pivotal air battle with the German Luftwaffe with Britain expecting an invasion. Pilots who fought in the battle have been known as The Few ever since; at times being specially commemorated on the 15th September, "Battle of Britain Day".
22nd	Harrow in northwest London received a German bomb at 3:30 a.m., the first to fall within the borders of the London Civil Defense Area.
23rd	King George VI commanded that the names of all Germans and Italians be stricken from the lists of British titles and decorations. The order affected Benito Mussolini, who had been made a member of the Order of the Bath in 1923, as well as King Victor Emmanuel III who had been a member of the Order of the Garter. No prominent Nazis were affected as few Germans held any British titles.
24th	The Luftwaffe dropped bombs on the financial heart of London and Oxford Street in the West End, probably unintentionally as the German bomber pilots had likely made a navigational error and did not know they were over the city. Winston Churchill was outraged at what he perceived to be a deliberate attack and ordered the RAF to bomb Berlin in retaliation.
25th	The RAF bombed Berlin for the first time in the war. Damage was slight and nobody was killed, but it came as a loss of face for Hermann Göring, who had boasted that Berlin would never be bombed. Hitler authorized the bombing of London in retaliation.
26th	No. 1 Fighter Squadron RCAF became the first Royal Canadian Air Force unit to engage enemy planes in battle when it encountered German bombers over southern England.
27th	President Roosevelt signed a joint resolution authorizing him to call National Guard and Army Reserve components into federal service for one year.
28th	The first major air raid on Liverpool took place in August 1940, when 160 bombers attacked the city on the night of the 28th August. This assault continued over the next three nights, then regularly for the rest of the year. There were 50 raids on the city during this three-month period. Some of these were minor, comprising a few aircraft, and lasting a few minutes, with others comprising up to 300 aircraft and lasting over ten hours. On the 18th September, 22 inmates at Walton Gaol were killed when high-explosive bombs demolished a wing of the prison.
31st	Film stars Laurence Olivier and Vivien Leigh were married at the San Ysidro Ranch in California.

September

1st | Biggin Hill aerodrome in Kent was heavily damaged by a German bombing raid.

4th | Hitler told a crowd at a rally in Berlin: "When the British air force drops two or three or four thousand kilograms of bombs, then we will in one night drop 150, 230, 300 or 400 thousand kilograms - we will raise their cities to the ground."

5th | Oil storage tanks at Thameshaven were among the day's targets of German bombers. Fires broke out at Thameshaven that could be seen from London.

8th | The Blitz began when the Luftwaffe shifted its focus from bombing British airfields and aircraft factories to conducting terror raids on London and other major cities in an effort to break the morale of the British people. This proved to be a mistake, as it would give RAF Fighter Command much-needed time to regroup.

11th | Winston Churchill gave a radio address saying that a German invasion of Britain could not be delayed for much longer if it was to be tried at all, so "we must regard the next week or so as a very important week for us in our history. It ranks with the days when the Spanish Armada was approaching the Channel and Drake was finishing his game of bowls, or when Nelson stood between us and Napoleon's Grand Army at Boulogne. We have read about all this in the history books, but what is happening now is on a far greater scale and of far more consequence to the life and future of the world and its civilization than those brave old days of the past. Every man and woman will therefore prepare himself and herself to do his duty whatever it may be, with special pride and care."

12th | U.S. Ambassador to Tokyo Joseph Grew warned Secretary of State Hull that Japan might treat an American embargo on oil exports as sanctions and retaliate.

15th | The large-scale air battle known as Battle of Britain Day was fought. Believing the RAF was near its breaking point, the Luftwaffe mounted an all-out offensive, sending two huge waves of about 250 bombers each to bomb London and surrounding areas. The RAF managed to scatter many of the German bomber formations and shoot down 61 planes while losing 31 in return, inflicting a clear and decisive defeat on the Germans.

16th | RAF planes from the carrier Illustrious attacked Benghazi and sank four Italian ships.

17th | Heinrich Himmler ruled that all Polish workers must wear a yellow badge marked with the letter "P" to distinguish themselves from Germans.

19th | The Royal Air Force bombed German invasion barges in ports along the French coast. After the attack, Hitler ordered the barges dispersed.

21st | The British government officially approved the use of the London Underground as an air-raid shelter, long after civilians had started using it as one anyway.

25th | Joachim von Ribbentrop alerted the German embassy in the Soviet Union that Japan was likely to join Italy and Germany in an alliance soon. Should this happen, the ambassador was instructed to reassure Moscow that this alliance was meant to deter the United States from entering the war and was not directed against Soviet interests?

September

26th The U.S. government placed an embargo on the exportation of scrap iron and steel to any country outside the Western Hemisphere excluding Britain, effective from the 16th October.

27th The Tripartite Pact, also known as the Berlin Pact, was an agreement between Germany, Italy and Japan signed in Berlin on the 27th September 1940 by, respectively, Joachim von Ribbentrop, Galeazzo Ciano and Saburō Kurusu. It was a defensive military alliance that was eventually joined by Hungary (20th November 1940), Romania (23rd November 1940), Bulgaria (1st March 1941) and Yugoslavia (25th March 1941), as well as by the German client state of Slovakia (24th November 1940). Yugoslavia's accession provoked a coup d'état in Belgrade two days later, and Germany, Italy and Hungary responded by invading Yugoslavia (with Bulgarian and Romanian assistance) and partitioning the country. The resulting Italo-German client state known as the Independent State of Croatia joined the pact on the 15th June 1941.

28th The first U.S. destroyers reached Britain.

29th British warships bombarded the coastal road of Italian Libya.

30th The day before the annual two-week autumn vacation, school children in Berlin were told that they would be granted extra vacation time if their parents wanted them to go to the country or accept invitations from relatives in rural areas.

October

3rd Neville Chamberlain stepped down as Lord President of the Council due to failing health.

4th Adolf Hitler and Benito Mussolini met at the Brenner Pass to discuss a strategy that included the possibility of Francoist Spain entering the war on their side. Mussolini had already decided to attack Greece and hinted at his intention by speaking scornfully of the attitude of the "double-dealing" Greek government, but Hitler brushed such talk aside and said that the Axis powers should avoid any initiative that was not "absolutely useful." Hitler did not reveal his intention to attack the Soviet Union.

October

6th | Mussolini made a surprise inspection of armed forces in northern Italy as the Fascist press predicted that "something big" was coming soon.

7th | The Royal Air Force conducted its heaviest raid on Berlin to date.

8th | The John Ford-directed drama film The Long Voyage Home starring John Wayne, Thomas Mitchell and Ian Hunter premiered at the Rivoli Theatre in New York City.

9th | Winston Churchill was elected head of the Conservative Party following the retirement of Neville Chamberlain.

11th | The British battleship Revenge and six destroyers bombarded Cherbourg. Philippe Pétain gave a radio address suggesting to the French people that they reconsider their historic view of who was friend and who was foe among the European nations.

13th | 14-year old Princess Elizabeth made her first public speech, a radio address to the children of the British Commonwealth. Her ten-year-old sister Princess Margaret joined in at the end.

14th | A German bomb exploded on the road above Balham station in south London, creating a large crater which a double-decker bus drove into during blackout conditions. A total of 66 people were killed and pictures of the bus in the crater were published around the world.

October

16th | Two Air Raid Precautions rescue workers were jailed for one year each at the Old Bailey for looting after they took £16 they found in a bombed-out house.

20th | Italian planes attacked oilfields in Bahrain and Saudi Arabia.

21st | Winston Churchill made a radio broadcast directed to the people of France. In a French-language address he appealed to them not to hinder Britain in the war against Germany, saying that "we are persevering steadfastly and in good heart in the cause of European freedom and fair dealing for the common people of all countries for which, with you, we draw the sword ... Remember, we shall never stop, never weary, and never give in, and that our whole people and empire have bowed themselves to the task of cleansing Europe from the Nazi pestilence and saving the world from the new Dark Ages."

23rd | President Roosevelt made a campaign speech in Philadelphia in which he answered many charges from his opponents, including one in particular that he called "outrageously false ... a charge that offends every political and religious conviction that I hold dear. It is the charge that this Administration wishes to lead this country into war." Roosevelt's speech concluded: "We are arming ourselves not for any foreign war. We are arming ourselves not for any purpose of conquest or intervention in foreign disputes. I repeat again that I stand on the platform of our party; 'We will not participate in foreign wars and will not send our Army, naval or air forces to fight in foreign lands outside of the Americas except in case of attack.' It is for peace that I have labored; and it is for peace that I shall labor all the days of my life."

25th | The Royal Air Force bombed Hamburg and Berlin.

28th | Hitler and Mussolini met in Florence to exchange the latest war information. Hitler might have intended to use the meeting to dissuade Mussolini from attacking Greece had the invasion not, as it turned out, gone ahead that morning. Mussolini was in high spirits and told Hitler, "Don't worry, in two weeks, it will all be over." Hitler wished Mussolini the best of luck and refrained from expressing any disapproval, though after the meeting he fumed to his inner circle that what Mussolini had done was "pure madness" and that he should have attacked Malta instead.

29th | The British occupied Crete and began to mine the waters around Greece.

31st | The Battle of Britain ended. Between August 8 and this date the Luftwaffe lost 2,375 planes while the RAF lost 800.

November

2nd | One of the most extraordinary aviation incidents of the war took place. Greek Air Force pilot Marinos Mitralexis, after running out of ammunition, rammed an Italian bomber. Mitralexis then landed his plane and captured the Italian crew who had parachuted to safety.

3rd | After enduring 57 consecutive nights of bombing since the Blitz began, London went a night without being bombed.

November

4th | Operation MB8 was a British Royal Navy operation in the Mediterranean Sea from the 4th to the 11th November 1940. It was made up of six forces comprising two aircraft carriers, five battleships, 10 cruisers and 30 destroyers, including much of Force H from Gibraltar, protecting four supply convoys.

5th | The German heavy cruiser Admiral Scheer located Allied convoy HX 84 in the North Atlantic and sank the British armed merchant cruiser Jervis Bay and five cargo ships.

7th | Irish Taoiseach Éamon de Valera rejected a British request that strategic naval ports and air bases on Irish territory be rendered or leased to Britain.

10th | The first aircraft to be ferried from Gander, Newfoundland to the United Kingdom took off. The formation of seven Lockheed Hudson bombers landed the next morning at Aldergrove, Northern Ireland after a 10-hour-17-minute flight. Over the course of the war some 10,000 aircraft would travel this route from North America to Europe.

11th | The Battle of Taranto began off Taranto, Italy. The Royal Navy launched the first all-aircraft ship-to-ship naval attack in history.

13th | The Handley Page Halifax is a British Royal Air Force four-engine heavy bomber of the Second World War. It was developed by Handley Page to the same specification as the contemporary twin-engine Avro Manchester.

November

14th	The Nazis legalized the human consumption of dog meat within the German Reich, effective from the 1st January.
16th	The RAF bombed Berlin, Hamburg, Bremen and other cities in retaliation for the Coventry bombing.
17th	The British attempted Operation White, an attempt to deliver fourteen aircraft from the carrier HMS Argus to Malta, but only five planes made it due to bad weather and the presence of the Italian Fleet.
19th	About 900 people were killed in a German bombing raid on Birmingham.
22nd	All Star Comics #3 was published, marking the debut of the first team of superheroes, the Justice Society of America.
23rd	Southampton Blitz: The first sustained air raid on Southampton occurred. 77 were killed and more than 300 injured.
25th	Woody Woodpecker made his debut in the animated short, Knock Knock.
26th	In the wake of the German–Soviet Axis talks, Vyacheslav Molotov told the German ambassador to the Soviet Union that the USSR was willing to join a four-power pact with Germany, Italy and Japan if new Soviet territorial demands were met, including expansion into the Persian Gulf and the annexation of Finland. Hitler called Stalin a "cold-blooded blackmailer" and refused to make any response to the Soviet proposal.
28th	The Germans bombed Liverpool and killed 166 civilians when a parachute mine caused a blast of boiling water and gas in an underground shelter.
29th	German military leaders issued a draft plan for the German invasion of the Soviet Union.
30th	A six-hour attack occurred in the Southampton Blitz, killing 137 people.

December

1st	Allied convoy HX 90 was sighted by German submarine U-101. The Germans would sink a total of 11 ships from the convoy from this day through to 3 December.
2nd	The British armed merchant cruiser Forfar was sunk west of Scotland by the German submarine U-99. The cargo ship Wilhelmina was torpedoed and sunk in the North Atlantic by the German submarine U-94.
4th	The swashbuckler film The Son of Monte Cristo starring Louis Hayward and Joan Bennett premiered at the Capitol Theatre in New York City.
6th	British submarine HMS Regulus was lost near Taranto, probably to a naval mine.
7th	The British Fairey Barracuda dive bomber plane had its first test flight.

December

7th   Ambassador Alfieri met with Adolf Hitler, who gave him a second lecture against Italy attacking Greece. Hitler said that Mussolini should resort to mobile courts-martial and executions if he wanted to turn the situation around. Hitler did agree to authorize fifty heavy troop transport planes to move fresh units from Italy to Albania.

8th   The British passenger and cargo steamship Calabria was torpedoed and sunk by the German submarine U-103 off County Galway, Ireland.

9th   Operation Compass was the first large Allied military operation of the Western Desert Campaign (1940–1943) during the Second World War. British and other Commonwealth and Allied forces attacked Italian forces in western Egypt and Cyrenaica, the eastern province of Libya, from December 1940 to February 1941. The Western Desert Force (Lieutenant-General Richard O'Connor) with about 36,000 men, advanced from Mersa Matruh in Egypt on a five-day raid against the Italian positions of the 10th Army (Marshal Rodolfo Graziani), which had about 150,000 men in fortified posts around Sidi Barrani in Egypt and in Cyrenaica.

The 10th Army was swiftly defeated and the British continued the operation, pursuing the remnants of the 10th Army to Beda Fomm and El Agheila on the Gulf of Sirte. The British took over 138,000 Italian and Libyan prisoners, hundreds of tanks, and more than 1,000 guns and aircraft, against British losses of 1,900 men killed and wounded, about 10 per cent of the infantry. The British were unable to continue beyond El Agheila, due to broken down and worn out vehicles and the diversion, beginning in March 1941, of the best-equipped units to the Greek Campaign in Operation Lustre.

12th   The first of four nights of heavy German bombing of Sheffield, England known as the Sheffield Blitz began.

14th   Plutonium was first isolated and produced at the University of California, Berkeley.
German submarine U-71 was commissioned.

15th   The ashes of Napoleon II were brought from Vienna to Paris, exactly one hundred years to the day since the retour des cendres when Napoleon Bonaparte's repatriated remains were interred at Les Invalides. The move was meant as a gesture of reconciliation on the part of Hitler, but a popular joke among the French went that the Parisians would have preferred coal to ashes.

16th   Bombing of Mannheim: The first area bombardment of a German city was conducted by the Royal Air Force when 134 bombers attacked Mannheim during the night, starting large fires on both banks of the Rhine.

17th   U.S. President Franklin D. Roosevelt gave a press conference in which he suggested leasing or selling of arms to Britain "on the general theory that it may still prove true that the best defense of Great Britain is the best defense of the United States, and therefore that these materials would be more useful to the defense of the United States if they were used in Great Britain, than if they were kept in storage here."

19th   German submarine U-37 mistakenly torpedoed and sank the Vichy French submarine Sfax and suppor ship Rhône off the coast of Morocco. The U-boat captain chose not to record this incident on the ship's logs.

December

20th	Two Spitfire fighters of No. 66 Squadron RAF attacked Le Touquet in France, strafing targets of opportunity such as power transformers. This tactic, codenamed Rhubarb, marked a shift in RAF tactics to a more offensive role.
21st	The RAF bombed docks and oil tanks at Porto Marghera, Italy.
22nd	The heaviest raids of the Manchester Blitz began. Over the next two days a total of 654 people were killed and over 2,000 injured.
23rd	Winston Churchill broadcast an appeal to the people of Italy, telling them to overthrow Mussolini for bringing them into a war against their wishes. "Surely the Italian army, which has fought so bravely on many occasions in the past but now evidently has no heart for the job, should take some care of the life and future of Italy?" Churchill asked. It is unlikely that many Italians heard the speech since they were forbidden from listening to foreign broadcasts.
24th	Mahatma Gandhi wrote his second letter to Hitler, addressing him as "Dear Friend" and appealing to him "in the name of humanity to stop the war. You will lose nothing by referring all the matters of dispute between you and Great Britain to an international tribunal of your joint choice. If you attain success in the war, it will not prove that you were in the right. It will only prove that your power of destruction was greater. Whereas an award by an impartial tribunal will show as far as it is humanly possible which party was in the right?"
25th	Near Beauvais, Adolf Hitler met with the French naval commander François Darlan. Hitler was in a foul mood and declared he was offering military collaboration with Vichy France one last time, and if France refused again it would be "one of the most regrettable decisions in her history."
29th	Superman co-creator Joe Shuster was arrested in Miami Beach, Florida for the "suspicious behavior" of looking into an automobile as if preparing to steal it. The following day he was sentenced to 30 days in prison until someone thought to give Shuster a pen and paper so he could prove his identity. Shuster drew a perfect illustration of Superman and the police let him go free.
30th	The famous photograph St Paul's Survives was taken of St Paul's Cathedral in London during the Second Great Fire of London.
31st	RAF bombers attacked Vlorë on the Greco-Italian front, Rotterdam and IJmuiden in the Nazi-occupied Netherlands and the German cities of Emmerich am Rhein and Cologne.
	Hitler issued a New Year's Order of the Day to Germany's armed forces, declaring "the year 1941 will bring us, on the Western Front, the completion of the greatest victory of our history."

PEOPLE IN POWER

Robert Menzies
1939-1941
Australia
Prime Minister

Philippe Pétain
1940-1944
France
Président

Getúlio Vargas
1930-1945
Brazil
President

William Mackenzie King
1935-1948
Canada
Prime Minister

Lin Sen
1931-1943
China
Government of China

Adolf Hitler
1934-1945
Germany
Führer of Germany

Marquess of Linlithgow
1936-1943
India
Viceroy of India

Benito Mussolini
1922-19543
Italy
President

Hiroito
1926-1989
Japan
Emperor

Manuel Ávila Camacho
1940-1946
Mexico
President

Joseph Stalin
1922-1952
Russia
Premier

Jan Smuts
1939-1948
South Africa
Prime Minister

Franklin D. Roosevelt
1933-1945
United States
President

Hubert Pierlot
1939-1945
Belgium
Prime Minister

Peter Fraser
1939-1949
New Zealand
Prime Minister

Sir Winston Churchill
1940-1945
United Kingdom
Prime Minister

Per Albin Hansson
1936-1946
Sweden
Prime Minister

Christian X
1912-1947
Denmark
King

Francisco Franco
1936-1975
Spain
President

Miklós Horthy
1920-1944
Hungary
Kingdom of Hungary

The Year You Were Born 1940
Book by Sapphire Publishing

Made in the USA
Monee, IL
13 October 2023

44519357R00055